Honor, Glory, Respect: Conducting Police Funerals, is the only book of its kind that I have found which comprehensively addresses the origins and practices of the traditional American police funeral. It is a must-read for anyone who is responsible for conducting these sacred and vital traditions in law enforcement.

> Captain Dan Rakofsky
> Florida

Much of married life with a law enforcement officer is spent in a state of denial; danger exists each day, and my greatest fear became my living nightmare. A police officer funeral is an experience that will haunt your memory for a lifetime; a book such as this is very informative to both law enforcement as well as civilians, to understand the dedication and discipline involved with serving the honor guard detail.

> Elizabeth Somohano, widow of
> MDPD Officer Jose Somohano

Every police administrator should have this book.

> Chief Max Chesterfield
> Mississippi

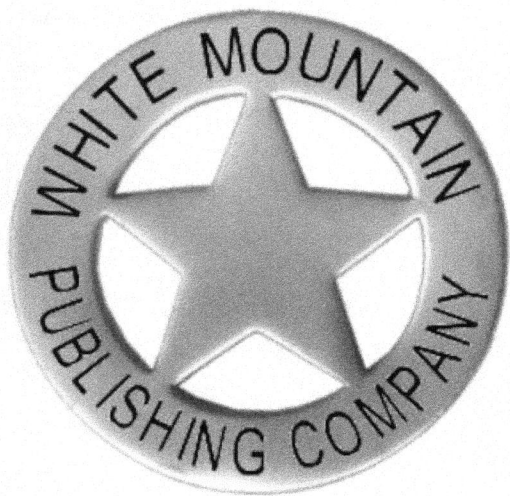

WHITE MOUNTAIN
WM
PUBLISHING COMPANY

Honor, Glory, Respect:
Conducting Police Funerals

A book by

Sgt. Michael W. Weissberg

WHITE MOUNTAIN PUBLISHING CO.

MIAMI, FLORIDA

2011

WHITE MOUNTAIN PUBLISHING CO.

MIAMI, FLORIDA

Copyright 2011 by Michael Weissberg

First edition (second printing)

Library of Congress Cataloging-in-Publication Data

Weissberg, Michael.

      Honor, Glory, Respect: Conducting Police Funerals by Michael Weissberg –
1st ed.

Library of Congress Control Number: 2011922202
ISBN-10 0983486603
ISBN-13 9780983486602

11 10 9 8 7 6 5 4 3 2

Book design by Michael Weissberg
Cover Photos of uniform & Ceremonial Bugle by Michael Weissberg

Printed in the United States of America

Be not ashamed of thy virtues; honor's a good brooch to wear in a man's hat at all times.

~ Ben Johnson

Our strength grows out of our weaknesses.

~ Ralph Waldo Emerson

About the Author

Michael W. Weissberg

Sergeant Weissberg began his career as an educator in 1988. A graduate of the University of Miami, Weissberg holds Master's degrees in Education and Criminal Justice from Nova Southeastern University and Florida International University, as well as a Graduate Certificate in Criminal Justice Administration and Policy Making.

Weissberg is currently pursuing a PhD in Psychology at Northcentral University, and has completed 19 doctoral level classes, and was awarded a Certificate of Advanced Graduate Study in Industrial Organizational Psychology with a focus on Law Enforcement Management.

Professor Weissberg has taught on the undergraduate level at Miami Dade College, St. Thomas University, and Florida International University, and graduate school at Nova Southeastern University. Weissberg has served as a professor for courses in the English, Education, and Criminal Justice Departments for these Schools.

Professor Weissberg has also taught inservice and Basic Law Enforcement Academy (BLE), Corrections Academy, Corrections-Law Enforcement Crossover Academy (COLE) at MDC, and was instrumental in developing the curriculum for the BAS program at Miami Dade College. Weissberg served as instructor for Driving, Crime Scene, Instruction [ITW], Public Speaking, Traffic Crash Reporting, and other subjects.

As a Law Enforcement Officer, Weissberg has been involved in DUI enforcement for nearly his entire career. Weissberg has arrested or assisted in the arrests of nearly 1000 impaired drivers, and is a veteran of over 2500 DUI investigations spanning most of Miami Dade County.

Sergeant Weissberg currently serves as DRE / DUI Coordinator, Agency Inspector, Breath Test Operator, Agency Inspector Instructor, Breath Test Operator Instructor, NHTSA DWI Certified Agency Inservice Instructor, and Drug Recognition Expert for the South Miami Police Department.

Weissberg has participated in many DUI Checkpoints,

Saturation Patrols, and Heightened Patrols for SMPD, and has served as Coordinator for every Multiagency DUI Checkpoint and Multiagency Saturation patrol hosted by SMPD from 2005 -2010, and served as Commander for many of these events. Weissberg has secured 12 grants totaling over $15,000 for DUI enforcement, and has written policy for the department.

Sergeant Weissberg's Instructors include Matthew Malhiot, Dr. Patrick Murphy, and Pete Beltran (Intoxylizer 8000), Dr. Carl Citek and Dr. Jack Richman (Eye Examinations), Mike Flarity, Jerry Davenport, Luis Blasco, Luis Taborda and Thomas Page (DRE Procedures), and Chip Walls (Toxicology).

Sergeant Weissberg also developed a strong background in investigations through his work and research as a student, instructor, professor, and investigator in the areas of General Investigations [GIU], Photography, Crime Scene [CSI], Traffic, Field Training Officer [FTO], Speed Measurement, and Traffic Homicide [THI].

Among his many certifications, Weissberg earned the coveted Florida Crime Prevention Practitioner designation [FCPP] from the Office of Attorney General Bob Butterworth, and was reaccredited by the Office of Attorney General Charlie Crist.

Sergeant Weissberg serves on the Miami-Dade County DUI Task Force, Miami-Dade County State Attorney's Office DUI Advisory Board, Mothers Against Drunk Driving Executive Board, and Advocate DUI Advisory Board and Executive Board. As DUI Coordinator for SMPD, Weissberg has been credited for a 40% increase in DUI arrests for 2005, 138% increase in DUI arrests for 2006, and an estimated 200% increase in DUI arrests for 2007.

Sergeant Weissberg has been awarded several commendations, including Officer of the Month [Kiwanis], Officer of the Quarter [Pinecrest Police Department], Lifesaving Award [Pinecrest Police Department], Officer of the Year 2000

[Pinecrest Business Association], Chief's Award 2006 [South Miami Police Department], Miami MADD Robbie Smith Memorial Award [DUI Officer of the Year 2006], Miami MADD Top Cop Award 2006, Dade Chief's Association's LEO Award 2006 [Public Safety Category], and was nominated for the Florida Police Chief's Association's Officer of the Year 2006.

As a detective, Weissberg was awarded the Unit citation in June of 2009. Weissberg was promoted to Police Sergeant in November of 2010 and assumed the responsibilities of Accreditation Manager, Grants Manager, Special Projects Director, DIU/DRE Supervisor, Honor Guard Supervisor, Firearms Unit Supervisor, and was temporarily detailed as Detective Sergeant in the Criminal Investigations Division.

Besides being trained in the manual of arms for the shotgun and M1, Weissberg has trained in the manual of arms for the Muzzle-loading British Long Land #1 Service Musket, and cannon. Weissberg is a graduate of the US National Parks Cannoneer School at St. Augustine, and fired muskets and cannon at the National Park at St. Augustine and the National Park at St. Simon's Island, and at Florida state parks at Key Biscayne, Olustee, and Bushnell.

As a member of the Honor Guard, Sgt. Weissberg attended the Broward County Honor Guard Academy twice. Sgt. Weissberg has attended dozens of police funerals, in Miami Dade, Broward, Palm Beach, Martin, Polk, Orange, and Monroe Counties, and served on or commanded honor guards, color guards, and firing parties.

Michael Weissberg and
Florida Governor Charlie Crist

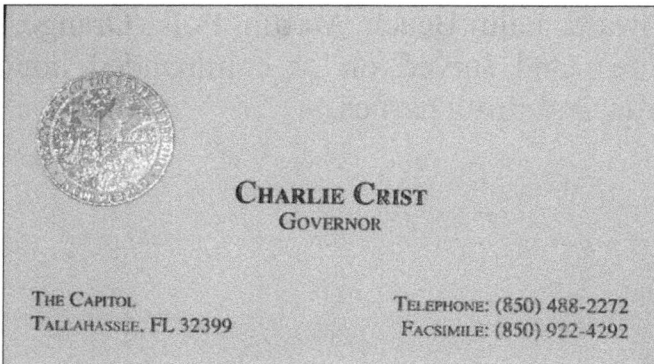

CHARLIE CRIST
GOVERNOR

THE CAPITOL
TALLAHASSEE, FL 32399

TELEPHONE: (850) 488-2272
FACSIMILE: (850) 922-4292

State of Florida Supreme Court
Tallahassee, Florida

Acknowledgements

Every now and then you have a teacher that is a true inspiration. Pete Beltran, Luis Blasco, Edwin Brodeur (deceased), Jerry Davenport, George Dillman, Scott Fingerhut, Mike Flarity, Bram Frank, Lester Goran, Wally Jay, Matthew Malhiot, Evelyn Wilde Mayerson, James Michener (deceased), Thomas Page, Clyde Pfleegor, Remy Presas (deceased), John Regan, Jack Richman, Don de Silva, Issac Bashevis Singer (deceased), Frank C. Stuart, Luis Taborda, Chip Walls, and Clark Zen are (were) those types of teachers.

For all of my students, past and present: I have taught you nothing. I have only shown you where to look. For all of the cops I have served with: be safe, do the right thing at the right time for the right reason, and the truth shall bear you up. Thank you for keeping me safe.

My grandfather, Sidney J. Weissberg was an inspiration. The wisdom, fairness, good judgment, and positivity that occasionally shows up in me, does so because it showed up in him daily.

My father, Steven M. Weissberg, M.D., is one of the most generous, funny, sarcastic, and wonderful people I have ever met. Any humor and personality that I have, I inherited from him. My father has supported my every educational goal and decision, both financially and emotionally.

My mother, Linda R. Weissberg, is a brilliant writer and teacher, and in the case of this book, a great editor. Even still, where she really excels is as a mother and grandmother.

It was my mother, together with my late great-aunt, Esther Berger, a caring librarian, taught me to love books, writing, and words.

My brother, Craig E. Weissberg, taught me about ethics, fair play, and doing the right thing. And he is a lawyer!

Last, my wife, Erika B. Weissberg. What did I ever do,

what god did I pray to, what streak of luck did I have, that I wound up with you? I hope you never wake up and realize that you are too good for me.

Dedication

The final resting place of
Officer Laverne "Daniel" Schulz

This book is dedicated to all fallen police officers everywhere; your sacrifice will never be forgotten. This book is specifically dedicated to the memory of Laverne "Daniel" Schulz. Officer Schulz was stabbed by juvenile gang members on November 27, 1987. Dan was attacked while working a uniformed off-duty job at a movie theater in the City of South Miami, Florida; he succumbed to his injuries a month later.

LAVERNE DANIEL SCHULZ
Badge 0023

CHARLES H. MANN
ALVIN V. KOHLER
CHERYL W. SEIDEN
ROBERT E. FITZPATRICK
LAVERNE DANIEL SCHULZ
JOSEPH P. MARTIN
LYNETTE HODGE
RUEBEN I. JONES

Section from the wall at the
Miami Dade County Police Memorial

The Officer Laverne "Daniel" Schulz
Monument in South Miami, FL
draped for a funeral

To honor Dan Schulz:

The National Law Enforcement Officers Memorial is the nation's monument to law enforcement officers who have died in the line of duty. Please donate. If you would like to contribute by phone, please call 202-737-3400.

NLEOMF
901 E Street NW, Suite 100
Washington, DC 20004-2025
info@nleomf.org
http://www.nleomf.org/officers/search/search-results/laverne-daniel-schulz.html

The Police Officer's Assistance Trust was founded in 1989 as a non-profit support organization for the law enforcement community of Miami-Dade County, Florida. To make a donation in the name of Laverne "Daniel" Schulz, contact POAT.

Police Officer's Assistance Trust
1030 NW 111 Avenue,
Miami, Florida 33172
305.594.6662
Email: poatoffice@msn.com

Prologue

I have been to dozens of funerals, and been an honor guard member, color guard member, casket guard, and a firing party member. I have been both a member and a commander. I didn't write this book because I am a great honor guard member; I can hardly march, slouch a bit, and I can name 3 dozen men and women who are more experienced honor guard members and who know more about this than I do, starting with my own department and including the instructors at the Broward County Honor Guard Academy.

I wrote this book only because no one else did. Accordingly, I had many honor guard gurus proofread this and tear it apart. If you find things wrong, let me know, and I will make corrections. I would be happy to put out a second edition. If I left things out, let me know; I would be happy to include them in a third edition, or a fourth, or a fifth. I did this for the officers and their families, because heroes never die, but the families still feel acute pain. This book is for them, and for you; not because I know so much, because I don't. It's because the public knows so little.

The best we can do, is the least we can do.

The Author

Special thanks go to the instructors and guest speakers at the 2011
Broward County Honor Guard Academy:

Ofc. Chris Stilwell, Plantation PD; Director
Capt. Denise Warrick, FWC; Asst. Director (Inst. Casket Carry)
Lt. Kim Dipre, FWC; (Inst. Casket Carry)
Lt. Rob Laubenberger, FWC; (Inst. Flag Presentation)
Ofc. Joe Brooks, FWC; (Inst. Flag Folding)
Ofc. Craig Boermeester, Plantation PD; (Inst. Flag Presentation)
Ofc. Ron Martin, Davie PD; (Inst. Manual of Arms)
Cpl. Tony Parvis (Ret.), Coconut Creek PD; (Inst. Manual of Arms)
Sgt. Al Butler, Plantation PD; (Inst. Rifle Volley)
Lt. Boris Millares, Hollywood PD; Treasurer, (Inst. Rifle Volley)
Sgt. Ed Chavez-Velando, Broward Sheriff's Office; (Inst. Casket Guard)
Mr. John Banas, Ft. Lauderdale Memorial Gardens (Inst. Casket Carry)
Ofc. Brandi Delvechio, Coconut Creek PD; Registrations & Secretary
Ms. Beatriz Stilwell, Plantation Fire/Rescue (Ret.); Photographer
Ms. Debbie Geary, COPS, South Florida Chapter (Speaker, Survivors)
Deputy Eric Strzlowski, COPS, South Florida Chapter (Speaker,
       Survivors)
Deputy Dave Campbell, Monroe County Sheriff's Office; Dist. 5 Pipe &
       Drum Corp. (Speaker, Bagpipes)
Capt. John Labendera, Ft. Lauderdale PD; (Speaker, "Taps" & Bugle)

Introduction

There is no formal police function that can match the pageantry and splendor of a police funeral. Why? It is necessary to promote healing, re-instill pride, and of course, to honor the dead.

Our job is a tough one. We sometimes feel that we are invincible. When an officer falls, it shatters the fragile shell of protection we must put up in order to do the things we do every day. When shots ring out, people fight, or violence erupts, the "normal" people run in the opposite direction. We run in that direction, lights blazing and sirens howling. We hardly ever think that we can get hurt or killed, but we can, and do. According to NLEOMF (2011), on average, one law enforcement officer is killed in the line of duty somewhere in the United States every 53 hours.

There are several units that are common to police funerals. Often some type of musical corps makes an appearance. A bagpipe and drum corps, redolent in the costumes of the Scotch or British Isles, pays homage to the days when police were comprised of Scottish, Irish, and English night watchmen. These units have pipers and drummers who perform with such precision and grace, that the onlookers can't help but feel pride and reverence. A bugler may play "Taps" in place of a bagpipe corps, if cost or access is a factor. It is easier to find a bugler than a bagpipe corps. A bugler can be hidden, so that a civilian may be utilized. The old military tradition of a second or an "echo bugler" may be used if desired.

An honor guard is resplendent in their Class A uniforms, often with special striping, pins, and shoulder cords or aiguillettes with fourgere tips. The honor guard will immediately on the death of a member lower the departmental American flag to half-mast. The Honor Guard may stand guard at the casket, one at the head, and another at the foot. The guard may be changed every fifteen minutes or every half-hour. The replacement guard will march slowly to the casket, salute, and relieve the guard. This additional ceremony pays honor to the dead.

A color guard presents the flags of the nation, state, and department. Riflemen, and in some cases, halberds or spontoons, may accompany the flags, and the detail may be commanded by a senior leader with a drawn sword.

Pallbearers, usually eight, may carry the casket, with ceremonial bearers who cannot heft the load, walking behind the pall in pairs, if desired.

The Chief Executive, Chief of Police, and / or Police Commissioner, act as dignitaries and usually do not participate, except to eulogize the dead if desired.

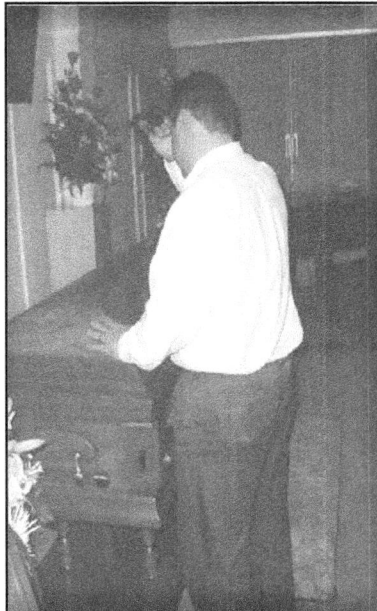

Bagpipes

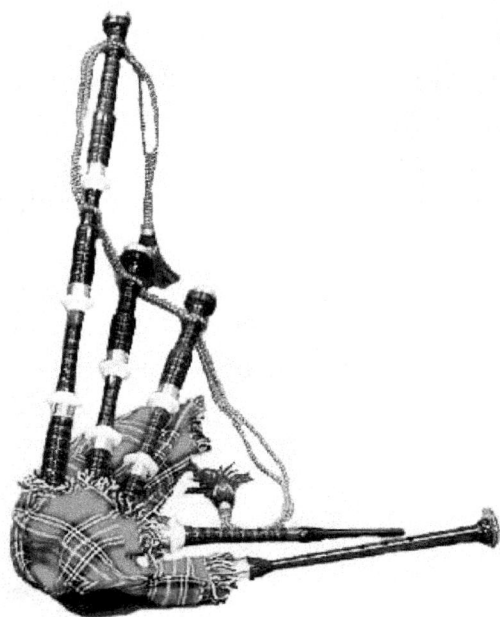

Music is an important part of any funeral service. The bagpipes have been commemorating the loss of loved ones with music at funeral services for hundreds of years. Many people associate bagpipes with funerals and this is because they powerfully touch our deepest emotions; the haunting voice of the bagpipe expresses feelings that words alone may fail to convey. The original use of bagpipes by the English, Irish, and Scottish were to inflame the passions of soldiers before battle, and to terrify enemies with the strange wailing notes.

Music choice is something that will have to be worked out with each piper. The Pipers will have several pieces of music that they will know and intend to play. The pipers will know a great number of tunes, but be sure to ask if you have a special request.

There are numerous compositions written specifically for the bagpipe for any occasion. The pipes have a narrow range of nine notes. As a result, most popular tunes cannot be played on this instrument.

The Minstrel Boy

The Minstrel Boy was written by Thomas Moore who set it to the melody of "The Moreen", an old Irish "aire" of unknown origin. Sheridan (2006) explains that the song tells of a musician-soldier who goes to war to seek revenge for the death of his father, carrying only his harp and his father's sword.

The minstrel boy is alone against the world, having been betrayed by all; he is captured, but destroys the strings of the harp so that it will not be played in slavery. The boy is killed, but his music lives on.

This is one of the most loved and most often used songs in police funerals. Many will recognize this song from "Star Trek: The Next Generation". The song's first verse was sung by the character Miles O'Brien (Colm Meaney) in the "Star Trek: The Next Generation" episode, "The Wounded", which originally aired January 28, 1991. The character sang the song "a cappella" in a haunting and memorable voice.

The Minstrel Boy
by Thomas Moore

The Minstrel Boy to the war is gone
In the ranks of death you will find him;
His father's sword he hath girded on,
And his wild harp slung behind him;
"Land of Song!" said the warrior bard,
"Tho' all the world betrays thee,
One sword, at least, thy rights shall guard,
One faithful harp shall praise thee!"

The Minstrel fell! But the foeman's chain
Could not bring that proud soul under;
The harp he lov'd ne'er spoke again,
For he tore its chords asunder;
And said "No chains shall sully thee,
Thou soul of love and brav'ry!
Thy songs were made for the pure and free,
They shall never sound in slavery!"

The Minstrel Boy
Third Verse

     The song originally consisted of two verses. As a result of its popularity, the song was a favorite of the many Irishmen who fought during the U.S. Civil War, primarily on the Union side. It was at this time that a third verse was added by unknown authors:

The Minstrel Boy will return we pray
When we hear the news
we all will cheer it,
The minstrel boy will return one day,
Torn perhaps in body, not in spirit.
Then may he play on his harp in peace,
In a world such as Heaven intended,
For all the bitterness of man must cease,
And ev'ry battle must be ended.

The Minstrel Boy
Concentrated Verse

The minstrel boy to the war is gone,
In the ranks of death ye may find him;
His father's sword he hath girded on,
With his wild harp slung along behind him;
Land of Song, the lays of the warrior bard,
May some day sound for thee,
But his harp belongs to the brave and free
And shall never sound in slavery!"

The instrument recognizable as the modern bagpipes may be as old as a thousand years, and may have existed during the crusades. The *New Oxford History of Music* makes mention of the first documented bagpipe being found on a Hittite slab at Eyuk in the Middle East. This sculptured bagpipe has been dated to 1000 BC. Other versions would be found around the world in the next thousand years.

The most common examples of modern bagpipes come from the 1700's and forward, but earlier examples and references are noted. A painting exists from the 15th century by Hieronymus Bosch, which shows bagpipers.

Chaucer's *Canterbury Tales* mention the bagpipes as early as 1386. There is even an International Bagpipe Museum in Gijón, Spain, which contains a trove of information, and examples from Europe, Africa, and Asia.

During the expansion period of the British Empire, British military forces included Highland regiments, and so the Scottish Great Highland Bagpipe became known worldwide.

Many civilians and officers alike know nothing about the bagpipes. Sheridan (2006) mentions that the pipes are reed instruments, like clarinets, but use air being pushed through to make the sound.

A chanter is a high pitched horn that works in tandem with a bass drone and two tenor drones. The piper puffs into a blowpipe to inflate the bag, then pumps the bag with the elbow crushing it against his ribs to push the air through, so the sound does not diminish while he breathes.

Irish pipes have one less drone. Pipes have been played all around the world, from Spain to Poland, Sweden to Hungary.

Many police departments and fire departments in England, Ireland, Scotland, Canada, Australia, Wales, New Zealand, Hong Kong, and the United States have also adopted the tradition of bagpipers, who play together with drums or fifes.

The Great Highland Bagpipe has also been adopted by

many countries that were formerly part of the British Empire, despite their lack of a Scottish or Irish population. These countries include India, Pakistan and Nepal. Sheridan (2006) states that many Americans first exposure to bagpipes was in the movie *Gunga Din*, when pipers marched with the British Army into India.

The British Army runs its own pipes and drums training facility, the Army School of Bagpipe Music and Highland Drumming, in Edinburgh, Scotland. To be qualified as a Pipe Major or Drum Major in the pipes and drums of a regiment of the British Army, candidates must successfully pass a series of courses at the school.

According to Sheridan (2006), The New York City Police Department's Emerald Society established a bagpipe band in 1960. The Fire Department of the City of New York followed suit in 1962, with members of the NYPD acting as instructors. The addition of pipers to the police funeral brings an ancient glory to the already spectacular event.

We owe it to our brave dead to make the police funeral the most spectacular, rich, and glorious event we put on. The hair stands up on the backs of the necks of all in attendance, when the chanters moan and the drones whine. The sound is slightly discordant and unnerving, which adds to the spectacle at the graveside, the same way it unnerved enemies hundreds of years ago on the field of battle.

"Amazing Grace" is a Christian hymn written by English poet and clergyman, John Newton (1725–1807), published in 1779. This is one of the best-known and best loved hymns, and is almost always piped at police funerals.

Amazing Grace
By John Newton

Amazing Grace, how sweet the sound,
That saved a wretch like me.
I once was lost but now am found,
Was blind, but now I see.
T'was Grace that taught my heart to fear.
And Grace, my fears relieved.
How precious did that Grace appear
The hour I first believed.
Through many dangers, toils and snares
I have already come;
'Tis Grace that brought me safe thus far
and Grace will lead me home.
The Lord has promised good to me.
His word my hope secures.
He will my shield and portion be,
As long as life endures.
Yea, when this flesh and heart shall fail,
And mortal life shall cease,
I shall possess within the veil,
A life of joy and peace.
When we've been here ten thousand years
Bright shining as the sun.
We've no less days to sing God's praise
Than when we've first begun.

Piper's Uniform

The police piper generally takes the uniform from the British Military Highland Regiments. The Highland regiment most well-known by Americans is the 42nd Royal Highland Regiment of Foote, the "Black Watch". The regiment served in 1745 in "The War of Jenkins' Ear", also known as "King George's War".

This war took place in Europe, as well as in Florida and Georgia, between the British and the Spanish. The 42nd was first moved to America, specifically New York in 1756, and served in America in the Revolutionary War.

The 42nd served in both World Wars, Korea, and was the last British regiment in Hong Kong before its return to China. Pipers take their uniforms in part from those worn by regiments such as this one.

Bagpipers are known by the spats, kilt, bonnet, sporran, and Culloden knife. The Culloden is also called the "Skian Dubhs" or "Skean Dhu" (pronounced "skian-doo") which means "black knife" in Gaelic. Typically, these knives were carried wedged in a stocking top in the style of the kilt-clad highland warriors.

The Skian Dubhs

The kilt is the most unusual part of the uniform. Its original form was that of a blanket wrapped around the body for warmth. Gradually it evolved into two pieces; the plaid (which is worn over the shoulder) and the kilt. A kilt consists of seven to ten yards of tartan with pleats in the back.

A Drum Major wears the formal dress and carries the crested mace, a symbol of leadership. Some pipers wear the busby, a symbol of Highlanders, and is almost identical to that worn by the guards at Buckingham Palace and Windsor Castle. These are sometimes made of bearskin. For headgear, some wear the Scottish bonnet, a soft beret-like hat.

The Horsehair Sporran

Sporrans are made of the skins of small fur-bearing animals. These are ornamental purses that allow the wearer to keep small items, since the kilt does not have pockets. Some police pipers wear shoulder patches on uniform shirts; some wear full gun belts.

Going Home

Going Home is another piper's tune that should be familiar to anyone who has attended police funerals. This march is played when the fallen officer is taken from the church.

Going Home is an old spiritual song based on an old man in his final days who sees his own death. This is another tune that is one of the most recognizable, and brings tears to the eyes of most everyone who hears it.

"Going Home"
Version 1

Going home, going home,
I'm just going home.
Quiet-like, slip away-
I'll be going home.
It's not far, just close by;
Jesus is the Door;
Work all done, laid aside,
Fear and grief no more.
Friends are there, waiting now.
He is waiting, too.
See His smile! See His hand!
He will lead me through.

Morning Star lights the way;
Restless dream all done;
Shadows gone, break of day,
Life has just begun.
Every tear wiped away,
Pain and sickness gone;
Wide awake there with Him!
Peace goes on and on!
Going home, going home,
I'll be going home.
See the Light! See the Sun!
I'm just going home.

"Going Home"
version 2

Many times in my childhood we'd travel so far
By nightfall how weary I'd grow.
Father's arms would slip 'round me and gently he'd say,
"My child, we're going home."

Going home, I'm going home.
There is nothing to hold me here.
I got a glimpse of that heavenly land;
Praise God, I am going home.

Now the twilight is fading, the day soon shall end,
I get homesick the farther I roam.
But the Father has blessed me each step of the way,
And now I am going home.

Going home, I'm going home.
There is nothing to hold me here.
I caught a glimpse of that heavenly land,
Praise God, we are going home.

Praise God, we are going home.

"Going Home"
version 3

Going home, moving on, through God's open door;
Hush, my soul, have no fear, Christ has gone before.
Parting hurts, love protests, pain is not denied;
Yet in Christ, life and hope span the great divide.
Going home, moving on, though God's open door;
Hush, my soul, have no fear, Christ has gone before.

No more guilt, no more fear, all the past is healed;
Broken dreams now restored, perfect grace revealed.
Christ has died, Christ is ris'n, Christ will come again;
Death destroyed, life restored, love alone shall reign.
Going home, moving on, through God's open door;
Hush, my soul, have no fear, Christ has gone before.

"Going Home"
version 4

Going home, going home,
I'm a going home.
Quiet-like, some still day,
I'm just going home.
It's not far, just close by,
Through an open door.
Work all done, care laid by,
Going to fear no more.
Mother's there, expecting me,
Father's waiting too.
Lots of folk gathered there,
All the friends I knew.

Nothing's lost, all's gain,
No more fear or pain,
No more stumbling by the way,
No more longing for the day,
Going to roam no more.

Morning star lights the way,
Restless dreams all done.
Shadows gone, break of day,
Real life has begun.
There's no break, there's no end,
Just a living on.
Wide awake with a smile,
going on and on.

Going home, going home,
I'm just going home.
It's not far, just close by,
Through an open door.
I am going home.
I'm just going home.

Going home, going home,
Going home, going home,
Going home.

The Bagpipes are versatile and can be used at almost any time in the service. The pipes can be played at the funeral home, leading the deceased out, or as a salute at the wake.

Pipes can be played at the church, piping into and out of the church, or part of the service. The pipes can be played at the cemetery, as a march to the grave or chapel, and after the ceremony, playing a salute. The tradition of a lone piper walking away while playing "Amazing Grace" and tapering off at the end while out of sight is called "piping them home".

Although piping is an Irish tradition, the Scottish great bagpipes are normally used. The Scottish highland bagpipes are louder than the traditional Irish uilleann pipes. Both types of pipes were used at funerals in the nineteenth century.

American Flag Etiquette

We take the stars from heaven,
the red from our mother country, sepa-
rating it by white stripes,
thus showing that we have separated
from her, and the white stripes shall go
down to posterity, representing
our liberty.

~ George Washington

The American Flag is the enduring symbol of our country. The flag of the United States is to be treated with the utmost respect. In the case of a funeral rite, the flag of the United States may be used to show respect for the deceased, but respect must be shown to the flag; it is not just an accessory for the funeral.

The measurement of a flag lengthwise is called the fly; the measurement of a flag widthwise is called the hoist. The United States Flag Code is found in Title 4 of the United States Code. According to Seeber (2008), the US Code governs the display and use of the flag, time and occasions for display, manner of display, and how to show respect for the flag. The US Code also grants authority to the President to modify the rules governing the flag.

There are many traditions associated with the flag. The spear point is the finial usually used when the flag is carried outdoors, and the eagle finial is normally used for indoors. The eagle should be positioned so that the eagle looks forward, and is not moving backwards, or "retreating".

According to Seeber (2008), the flag is usually lifted from the coffin and folded during, or immediately following, the 3-volley rifle salute and the sounding of "Taps". Placing spent shell casings into the fold of a Military Funeral Flag violates provisions of the United States Flag Code; in police funerals, this is a custom that is usually followed even though the US Code prohibits it.

Seeber (2008) states when used to drape the casket, the flag should be placed correctly. When used to drape a closed casket, the flag should be so placed that the union is at the head and over the left shoulder of the deceased.

When used to drape a half-couch open casket, the flag should be placed in three layers to cover the closed half of the casket in such a manner that the blue field will be the top fold, next to the open portion of the casket on the deceased's left.

When the flag is used to drape a full-couch casket, it should be folded in a triangular shape and placed in the center part of the head panel of the casket cap, just above the left shoulder of the deceased. During a funeral, the flag which was used to drape the casket, is held waist high over the grave by the pallbearers and immediately folded after the rifle volley and the sounding of "Taps". The flag should never be lowered into the grave or allowed to touch the ground.

Flags Flown over the US Capitol

Departments may purchase flags that have been flown over the United States Capitol in Washington, DC by petitioning their Senators or Representatives. A certificate signed by the Architect of the Capitol shows that the flag has flown over the capitol.

Tricorn Folded Flag

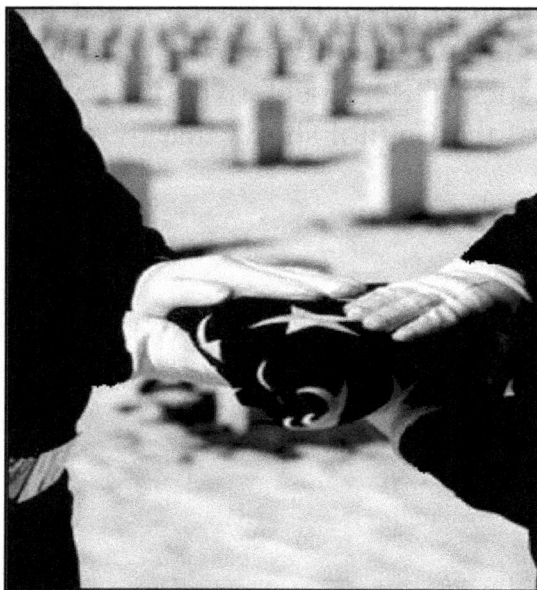

Where liberty dwells, there is my country.

~Benjamin Franklin

The custom of draping the casket with the national flag began during the Napoleonic Wars (1796-1815). Soldiers covered the dead with flags before carrying them from the field of battle on caissons.

This tradition was also carried though in the navy, where sailors killed would be wrapped in their own hammocks, sewn in, with the final stitch through the nose, to ensure the person was really dead.

The nation's flag would be then tucked in around the hammock-shroud. When the corpse was "consigned to corruption" and tipped overboard, the flag would be held and retained, and the body left to fall due to gravity.

A casket band is used to keep the flag from blowing away, since the casket is usually slick or polished, and the flag is cotton. An outdoor nylon flag is not used.

United States flags are placed on the casket so the union field is at the head and over the left shoulder. The flag is not placed in the grave and is not allowed to touch the ground.

During a police funeral, the honor guard formally folds the flag into a triangle. The blue field or "union" shows all around. This is symbolic of the tricorn hat or "cocked hat" our revolutionary war forefathers wore.

Soldiers under command of General George Washington, and sailors under command of Captain John Paul Jones wore cocked hats similar to the ones the British wore, but without the black rosette or "cockade" of the House of Hanover.

The flag is folded 12 times. The commander is in charge of receiving the flag; he will accept or reject the fold. If rejected, it may have to be re-folded. The flag fold must be tight and crisp, with only the union showing.

Sometimes, the fold is so tight, that when the honor guard passes the flag to the commander, and he holds it, the guard tucking the final edge may lose a white glove in the flag! If so, the flag will have a white glove inside. It is not a tradition to insert a white glove in the fold.

It is, however, a custom to place shells from the three volley salute in the final fold as a symbol of farewell to the warrior.

The commander then presents the flag to the Chief of Police. The flag is carried point down, to the chest, with the arms crossed. The commander presents the flag to the Chief, who then presents it to the "chief mourner" or next of kin.

The order of priority is spouse, then child, then parent, then grandparent. If no next of kin is present, a close friend may receive it. The Chief then says words to the effect of, "On behalf of a grateful nation, we present you with this flag as a token of our appreciation," or "On behalf of a grateful nation, community, and department, we present you this flag, with our condolences."

Another version of this is to say "On behalf of the Governor of the State of Florida and the Lake Erika Police Department, we present you this flag, with our thanks and condolences."

Seeber (2008) states that after a flag has been used for a funeral, it should never be flown again or displayed in any other way than in the tri-fold shape in which it was presented to the next of kin.

The folded flag should never be "opened" again. This is a sad, solemn, and beautiful tradition. There are many appropriate display cases available for purchase to display the burial flag and to protect it from wear and fading.

The department may present a triangle glass case to keep the flag in. It is recommended that at least one flag and case be kept on hand in the event it is needed.

The Officer's Boots

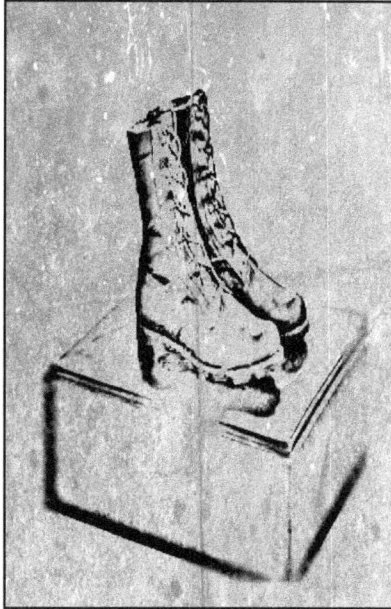

The effect of having the honor guard perform their solemn duties with care and precision shows how much we care for our comrades in arms, as well as for the communities and families they represent.

~Major General
Robert Ivany

According to the Department of the Army (2003), if asked to serve as a member of a funeral detail, remember, this service is for a deceased hero, and there are people present who will take comfort in a professional attitude and performance.

The police borrow from the military in these matters. While some traditions are timeless, others are newer. A more recent tradition is to display the officer's boots on a raised box of some type, possibly with a photo of the officer. If the officer's boots are unavailable, a pair of new or used boots can be obtained for the purpose of the display. Of course, it is best if the officer's boots can be obtained.

If the officer never wears boots, and wears shoes, brogans, or sneakers, then a pair of boots can be obtained. It is better to try to get a pair that is similar in size to the officer's. It would be ridiculous to use a pair of size 12 men's boots for a petite female's funeral.

This tradition is relatively new in the police world. In the Army and other branches of the U.S. military, some units prepare a visible reminder of the deceased soldier with a display of a pair of combat boots and an inverted rifle with the soldier's helmet and dog tags hanging on it. This is sometimes called a "battle cross" or the "soldier's battle cross". Many policemen are veterans of military service, and like the idea of displaying an officer's boots.

In the US Army, the helmet and identification tags signify the fallen soldier. The inverted rifle with bayonet signals a time for prayer and a break in the action to pay tribute to the dead. The combat boots represent the final march of the last battle. The rifle and helmet are not appropriate for police, except perhaps in the case of a SWAT officer. The Chief of Police should be consulted in this case.

An alternate tradition is to have the officer's hat on a pedestal which has been draped in black crepe.

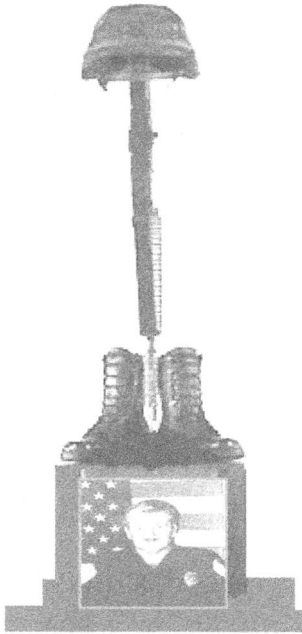

Rifle Volley

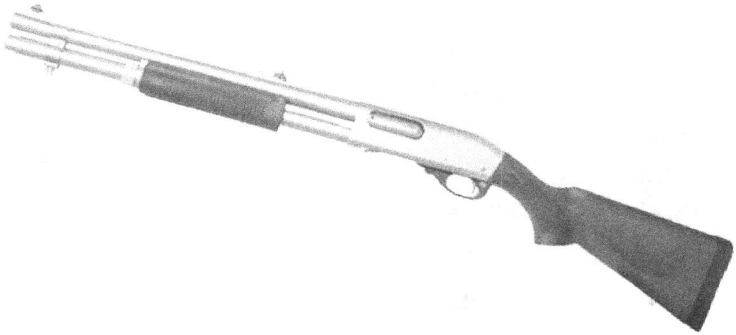

The tradition of firing three rifle volleys over the grave is different from a 21-gun salute. The rifle volley originated in the old custom of halting the fighting to remove the dead from the battlefield.

Once each army had cleared its dead, it fired three volleys to indicate the dead had been cared for and they were ready to go back to the fight.

The rifle volley firing party consists of three to seven riflemen, but that does not constitute a "21-gun salute". The 21-gun salute is the highest honor a nation renders and is fired in honor of a national flag, or the the sovereign or chief of state of a foreign nation.

The police funerary volley is three rounds. Blanks are always used for the volley by the firing party. The muzzles should be aimed in a way that fires over the casket. The commander must ensure that the rifle party does not point toward or over the bugler. The bugler must not be deafened.

The hardest part of the volley is racking the shotgun slides and firing the rounds so that it sounds like one gun firing.

The use of seven guns is common. The more guns used the more possibility that the firing will be ragged.

The Remington Model 870 shotgun is by far the most often used in firing volleys. Shotguns made by Smith and Wesson, Mossberg, Winchester, and Benelli are also popular with police departments.

The Colt AR-15 and clones, M1 Garands, and M14 Springfield rifles are also common. Sometimes a shell or shells are retained for addition into the tricorn folded flag as a mark of respect.

A member of the firing party may break formation and retrieve the spent casings. These fired casings can be used for the tradition, or pre-fired casings can be used.

There is a debate as to whether the casings should be tucked into the flag in this manner. Some say this is a violation of flag etiquette. This, like other traditions, is often disparaged when it is new, and gradually it becomes a cherished tradition.

The individual department may decide what is appropriate.

"Taps"

"Taps" was composed by General Daniel Adams Butterfield composed for his brigade (Third Brigade, First Division, Fifth Army Corps, Union Army of the Potomac) in July, 1862. Butterfield was awarded the Medal of Honor for actions during the Battle of Gaines Mill.

"Taps" is an incredibly beautiful piece of music. The original was an instrumental. Several popular versions of the words exist, but those listed below are the most popular. Villanueva (2011) states that "of all the military bugle calls, none is so easily recognizable or more apt to render emotion than the call "Taps". The melody is both eloquent and haunting and the history of its origin is interesting and somewhat clouded in controversy."

"Taps" is traditional at military funerals. Villanueva (2011) further says that the first sounding of "Taps" at a military funeral is commemorated in a stained glass window at The Chapel of the Centurion (The Old Post Chapel) at Fort Monroe, Virginia. The window, made by R. Geissler of New York, and based on a painting by Sidney King, was dedicated in 1958, and shows a bugler and a flag at half staff. This monument to "Taps" was erected by the Virginia American Legion and dedicated on July 4, 1969.

Horace Lorenzo Trim Version:

Day is done, gone the sun,
From the hills, from the lake,
From the sky.
All is well, safely rest,
God is nigh.

Version 2, Unknown Author:

Go to sleep, peaceful sleep,
May the soldier or sailor,
God keep.
On the land or the deep,
Safe in sleep.

Version 3, "John Wayne Version":

Fading light
Falling night
Trumpet call, as the sun, sinks in fright
Sleep in peace, comrades dear,
God is near.

Version 4, Unknown Author:

Thanks and praise, for our days,
'Neath the sun, neath the stars,
'Neath the sky,
as we go, this we know,
God is nigh.

Version 5, Unknown Author:

Fading light dims the sight,
And a star gems the sky, gleaming bright.
From afar drawing nigh -- falls the night.

Version 6, Unknown Author:

Then good night, peaceful night,
Till the light of the dawn shineth bright,
God is near, do not fear -- Friend, good night.

There is a new product on the market that can help a department add a bugler, when there is no one in the agency who can play. The "Ceremonial Bugle" is manufactured and offered for sale.

According to the website, The Ceremonial Bugle was developed by Simon Britton, Vice President of S & D Consulting. Mr. Britton is a consultant from Newcastle upon Tyne, England, who moved to the United States thirteen years ago. Based in New York City, S & D Consulting seeks to enhance people's lives through the application of emerging technologies.

The bugle is a real bugle with an insert that plays "Taps"; the officer only has to stand still and "fake it". Historically, the bugler stands far away in a manner as to be shown in silhouette.

According to their literature, "The device slides snugly deep into the bugle's bell. The device plays a high-quality recorded version of ""Taps"," taken from the 1999 Memorial Day service at Arlington National Cemetery. The resonating tones inside the bugle create a realistic horn quality. The "Ceremonial Bugle" operates on two 9 volt batteries." I would recommend using fresh batteries for each funeral.

The "American Ceremonial Bugle" in nickel silver is a 17 inch bugle, shipped with a silver insert that plays ""Taps" " and other calls. The bugle ships with a hard shell carry case. The price is steep at $525, but worth it. For more information go to www.ceremonialbugle.com or call (212) 426-3268.

I have no connection whatsoever to this company. I don't even own one of these, but I got to use one at the Broward County Honor Guard Academy in 2010, and again in 2011. It was impressive.

I first heard it during the manual of arms class for the M1 Garand, and I believed someone was playing, and I thought, "Wow, that player is good!" I think this is a great product, and I recommend it. The only drawback is that you cannot do the echo with this item.

I personally do not like, nor recommend the echo, unless the two buglers have practiced together extensively.

The Single Riderless Horse

"I can make a General in five minutes but a good horse is hard to replace."

~Abraham Lincoln

The single riderless horse that follows the caisson with boots reversed in the stirrups, is called the "caparisoned horse," in reference to its ornamental coverings, which have a detailed protocol all to themselves.

By tradition, in military funeral honors, a caparisoned horse follows the casket of an Army or Marine Corps officer who was a colonel or higher, or the casket of a president, by virtue of having been the nation's military commander in chief.

This is another custom new to police funerals. Any officer, regardless of rank, when killed in the line of duty, can have this honor. Even if the officer has never been in a mounted unit, or if the department has no mounted unit, the horse can still be used.

The riderless horse can be borrowed from another department, with the horse's rider used as a "groom" to lead the horse, with the rider's own boots turned backward. This tradition is simply a mark of respect and part of the pageantry.

The custom of the riderless horse is believed to date back to the time of Genghis Khan, when a horse was sacrificed to serve the fallen warrior in the next world. The caparisoned horse later came to symbolize a warrior who would ride no more.

Abraham Lincoln was the first U.S. president to be honored with a caparisoned horse at his funeral, when he was killed in 1865.

In ancient times, the horse would be killed and buried with its owner. The idea behind that custom was in keeping with the Egyptian idea of burying everything a pharaoh might need with him in his afterlife. The fallen warrior would have the use of the horse in the afterlife.

One might have seen the use of the caparisoned horse in Ronald Wilson Reagan's funeral, or the use of the riderless horse in John Fitzgerald Kennedy's funeral.

How to Nominate a Fallen Officer To State and National Memorials

Once the funeral is over and the family is provided with the necessary assistance, the department should nominate the officer to be honored by the Officer Down Memorial Page, Inc., the National Law Enforcement Officers Memorial Fund, Inc., and the state memorial in the state in which the officer was killed (not all states have state-level memorials).

Submitting an Officer to
The Officer Down Memorial Page, Inc.

These instructions are provided to assist with submitting an eligible officer to be honored on the Officer Down Memorial Page, Inc. Following the instructions will allow staff members to quickly conduct the necessary research in order to verify a line of duty death and have the officer added to the Officer Down Memorial Page.

Updating an Officer
Currently Honored On The
Officer Down Memorial Page

If the officer is already honored on the Officer Down Memorial Page, please locate his/her memorial and click on the "Update This Memorial" button on the bottom of the memorial.

Submitting an Officer
Killed This Year

For officers killed in the line of duty during the current year, please complete the online submission form. Please include a detailed synopsis of the incident and links to any news websites or other relevant websites with information about the death.

Submitting an officer killed
Prior to this year

Officers killed in the line of duty prior to the current year are considered historic cases and must be handled by the research department.

Please complete the online submission form with the details you have about the incident. You will then be contacted by an ODMP researcher with additional instructions. Before a historic officer will be added to the ODMP, the information must be verified through documentation such as newspaper articles and/or official documents. This information can be sent by mail or fax:

Officer Down Memorial Page, Inc.
PO Box 1047
Fairfax, VA 22038-1047
Fax: (786) 551-8562

National Law Enforcement
Officers Memorial
Nomination and Approval Process

An officer data form must be completed for each officer considered for inclusion on the Memorial. The form must be signed by the head of the agency for which the officer worked; forms that do not have the signature of an agency head will not be processed. Individuals not affiliated with the agency in which the officer served, may initiate an officer data form, but the form still must be signed by the agency head.

Officer data forms and any supporting documentation, are reviewed for accuracy and completeness by the memorial fund's research department. If additional information or documentation is needed, research staff will contact the submitting agency. Officers' data forms must be submitted to the research department by December 31st to be considered for inclusion on the Memorial the next year.

Completed forms are forwarded to a committee of the memorial fund board of directors called the names committee. Committee members thoroughly review each case to determine if the circumstances of the death meet the criteria for inclusion on the national Memorial.

During two or three meetings held at the beginning of each year, the committee votes to either approve or deny a case, or to send the case back to the submitting agency for more information. A case that has been denied by the committee can be re-submitted for consideration in future years, provided that additional information or documentation is supplied.

Once cases have been approved by the names committee, the memorial fund research staff contacts the agencies for which the officers worked, for confirmation and follow up. Staff also works with the Memorial's engravers to align the names on the Memorial and schedule the engraving, usually 2-3 weeks prior to National Police Week. Each May 13th, during the candlelight vigil at the Memorial, the newly engraved names are read aloud and formally dedicated on the monument.

Criteria for Inclusion

As defined by the National Law Enforcement Officers Memorial, "law enforcement officer" means an individual involved in crime control or reduction and who is directly employed on a full-time basis by a local, county, state or federal law enforcement agency of the United States or its territories, with or without compensation, who is duly sworn and has full arrest powers.

A law enforcement agency is a governmental agency or subunit thereof having statutory powers of arrest and involved in crime control or reduction. The agency must employ at least one full-time, duly sworn, trained and certified officer with full arrest powers, or the equivalent in part-time officers.

Officers serving with private or state colleges and universities, and railroads will also be included, provided they are recognized as having law enforcement status by state, U.S. or District of Columbia Code, are duly sworn, trained and certified, with full arrest powers.

In addition, military police officers will be included but only if, at the time of their death, they were experiencing similar hazards and performing similar duties as those normally experienced and performed by non-military law enforcement personnel.

In such cases, eligibility will be determined after a review of several issues, including, but not limited to, whether the officer was receiving combat, imminent danger, or hazardous pay, whose job description includes whether the officer was responding to a law enforcement violation in his or her area of jurisdiction, as well as the circumstances of death. Military police officers serving in a combat situation will not be included.

Less than full-time law enforcement officers will also be considered. In such cases, eligibility will be determined after a review of several issues, including, but not limited to, job description, training and circumstances of death.

Correctional employees shall be included if they are recognized as having law enforcement status by their employing jurisdiction. Other correctional employees who do not have formal law enforcement status but who do have a primary or limited responsibility for the custody and security of suspected or convicted criminal offenders, and are employed by a local, county, state or federal correctional agency, will also be considered.

"Line of duty" means any action which an officer is obligated or authorized by law, rule, regulation, or written condition of employment service, to perform, or for which the officer is compensated by the public agency he or she serves.

The term "killed in the line of duty," means a law enforcement officer has died as a direct and proximate result of a personal injury sustained in the line of duty. This includes victim law enforcement officers who, while in an off-duty capacity, act in response to a law violation. It also includes victim law enforcement officers who, while in an off-duty capacity, are en route to or from a specific emergency or responding to a particular request for assistance; or, the officer is, as required or authorized by law or condition of employment, driving his or her employer's vehicle to or from work; or when the officer is, as required by law or condition of employment, driving his or her own personal vehicle at work and is killed while en route to or from work.

Not included under this definition are deaths attributed to natural causes, except when the medical condition arises out of physical exertion, while on duty, that is required by law or condition of employment including, but not limited to, the following:

running or other types of exercise being performed as part of training programs administered by the employing agency

fitness tests administered by the employing agency

lifting of heavy objects or

a specific stressful response to a violation of law or an emergency situation causing an officer's death immediately or within 24 hours of violation or emergency situation, or causing his or her death during a continuous period of hospitalization immediately following the specific response to the specific stressful response to the violation of law or emergency situation.

Stressful responses include, but are not limited to, the following:

a physical struggle with a suspected or convicted criminal

performing a search and rescue mission that requires rigorous physical activity

performing or assisting with emergency medical treatment

responding to a violation of the law or emergency situation that involves a serious injury or death or

a situation that requires either a high speed response or pursuit on foot or in a vehicle.

Also not included under this definition are deaths attributed to voluntary alcohol or controlled substance abuse, deaths caused by the intentional misconduct of the officer, deaths caused by the officer's intention to bring about his or her own death, and deaths attributed to an officer performing his or her duty in a grossly negligent manner at time of death.

Each death caused by disease shall be reviewed by the Armed Forces Institute of Pathology or other medical personnel with similar skill and expertise. If it is determined that the officer died as a result of infectious disease contracted while performing official duties, or by exposure to hazardous materials or conditions, while performing official duties, that officer is eligible for inclusion on the Memorial.

An officer shall be included if a department states that the officer died in the line of duty, and there is no information to believe otherwise. The Memorial Fund Research staff shall exhaust all possible means available to verify an officer's eligibility status, and the correct spelling of the name. Efforts will include having the name verified by the law enforcement agency of record and a surviving family member.

A Note about the Criteria
for Adding Names to the Memorial

The criteria for including an officer's name on the National Law Enforcement Officers Memorial are separate and distinct from the line-of-duty death criteria used by other entities or programs, including state and local law enforcement memorials and the Public Safety Officers' Benefits (PSOB) Program, U.S. Department of Justice. Acceptance for inclusion on the National Law Enforcement Officers Memorial in no way impacts decisions made by the federal government regarding the awarding of PSOB benefits. For more information about PSOB, visit www.psob.gov or call 1-888-744-6513.

Members of the Miami Dade Fire Department deploy colors

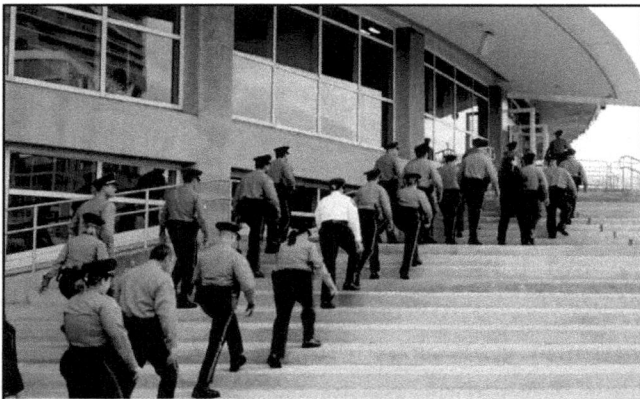

Miami Dade Police Offices at the American Airlines Arena for
the funeral of Amanda Howarth and Roger Castillo

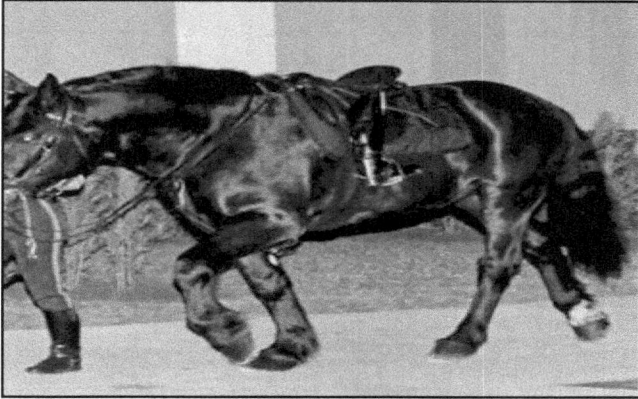

The riderless horse

Mounted honor guard

Procession for the Howarth - Castillo funeral

A homeless man in a wheelchair wrapped in the flag
watches a funeral procession

Civilians watch a funeral procession

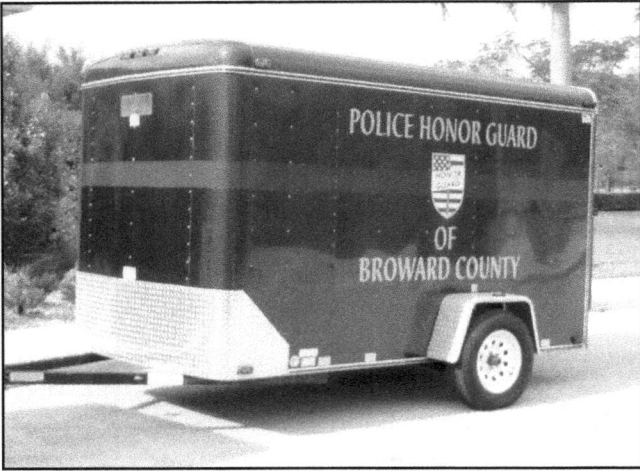

The Multiagency Honor Guard trailer

Honor Guard and Motormen
waiting for the Casket Coach

Waiting to escort fallen officers to the cemetery

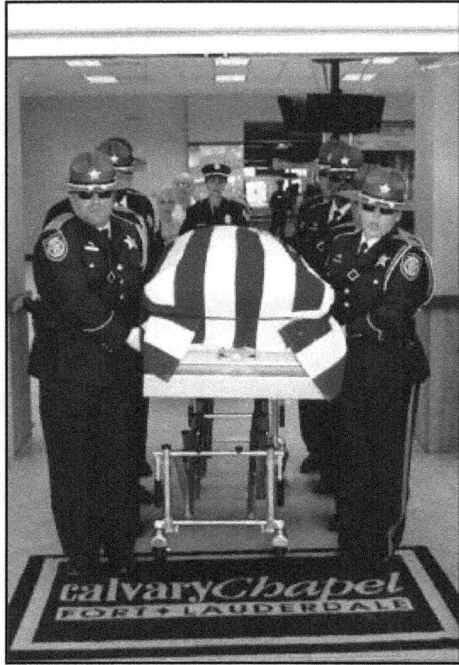

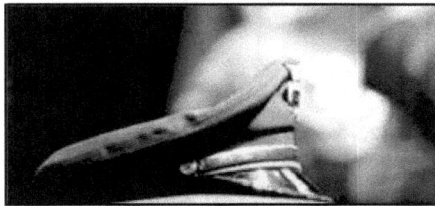

Amanda Howarth's hat

Florida Wildlife Conservation Commission
uses magnetic signs to convert their badge logo
to an honor guard logo

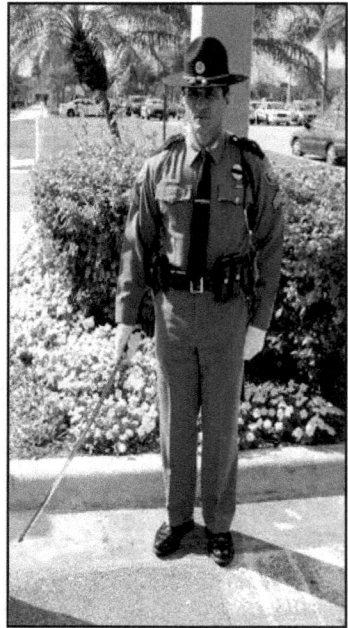

Funerals for Service Animals

Service animals generally include police canine dogs, nick-named "K9", and police horses. These wonderful animals live only to serve. A police dog may be trained to detect drugs, bombs, guns, or cadavers. The dogs may be trained for tracking or handler protection.

German Shepherd and Belgian Malinois are among the most popular for police work, but Bloodhounds, Beagles, Labradors, Spaniels and other dogs are used for detection work.

Police dogs believe that what they do is actually play. When the dog is successful, the handler gives the dog a treasured toy. The dog knows when it is time to go to work.

Mounted police use horses for crowd control and patrol. Some of the more famous uses of police horses include the Royal Canadian Mounted Police, The United States Border Patrol, the New Orleans Police Department in the French Quarter in New Orleans, and the City of Miami Police Department.

Harming a police service animal in many states is the same as harming a police officer.

Honoring these animals serves the same function as honoring a police officer. Many cities have monuments to their fallen service animals.

The partner of a service animal killed in the line of duty goes through many of the same feelings as the spouse of a fallen officer.

Possibly the biggest funeral in the history of the State of Florida was that of Matt Williams and his K9 partner DIOGI (pronounced "D-O-G"). Polk County Deputy Vernon Matthew "Matt" Williams and his partner were shot and killed on a traffic stop September 28th, 2006.

The subject was killed in a standoff with SWAT team members. SWAT fired 110 rounds at the subject when he pointed a gun at police. The subject was hit 68 times. When asked on FOX News Live, why he was shot 68 times, Polk County Sheriff Grady Judd stated "that's all the bullets we had".

Prayers

It is very important to find out in advance to what religion or sect an officer subscribed. There are many differences in the funerals for different religions. Catholic, Protestant, Muslim, Jewish, Church of God, Native American, and other faiths have rules and directives.

It would be easy to offend a family by offering a prayer that is inconsistent with the religion of the deceased. Some things that seem very normal and usual to one religion might be forbidden in another religion. It is paramount to remember that the service is mostly for the living.

Although we get very protective of the deceased officer, one must remember that the funeral is more for the living than the dead. The dead are free from the cares of this world. We do not want to offend. Remember, there is a reason that we render a hand salute to the surviving family.

Knowing this, the following prayers are reproduced. Inclusion should be based on the desires of the family and the deceased officer's wishes.

Reproduced here are the 23rd Psalm, the Lord's Prayer, and the Mourner's Kaddish.

23rd Psalm

The Lord is my Shepherd; I shall not want.
He maketh me to lie down in green pastures:
He leadeth me beside the still waters.
He restoreth my soul:
He leadeth me in the paths of righteousness for His name'
sake.
Yea, though I walk through the valley of the shadow of death,
I will fear no evil: For thou art with me;
Thy rod and thy staff, they comfort me.
Thou preparest a table before me in the presence of mine
enemies;
Thou annointest my head with oil; My cup runneth over.
Surely goodness and mercy shall follow me all the days of my
life,
and I will dwell in the House of the Lord forever.

The Lord's Prayer

Our Father, who art in heaven,
hallowed be thy name.
Thy Kingdom come,
Thy will be done,
on earth as it is in heaven
Give us this day our daily bread.
And forgive us our trespasses,
As we forgive those who trespass against us.
And lead us not into temptation,
But deliver us from evil.
For Thine is the kingdom,
and the power and the glory,
for ever and ever.
Amen.

Taken from the Anglican Book of Common Prayer, 1662.

Mourner's Kaddish

English Translation

Glorified and sanctified be God's great name throughout the world which He has created according to His will. May He establish His kingdom in your lifetime and during your days, and within the life of the entire House of Israel, speedily and soon; and say, Amen.

May His great name be blessed forever and to all eternity.

Blessed and praised, glorified and exalted, extolled and honored, adored and lauded be the name of the Holy One, blessed be He, beyond all the blessings and hymns, praises and consolations that are ever spoken in the world; and say, Amen.

May there be abundant peace from heaven, and life, for us and for all Israel; and say, Amen.

He who creates peace in His celestial heights, may He create peace for us and for all Israel; and say, Amen.

In Rocky III, Rocky Balboa recites the Mourners' Kaddish for Mickey. This is the first exposure most non-Jews have to this prayer. The prayer is normally said in Hebrew, which is a tricky tongue to pronounce.

The Jewish scholars have developed a transliteration, which allows us to sound out Hebrew using English letters. It is almost impossible to say the prayer in transliterated Hebrew without practice.

The Jewish funeral has many traditions, and varies among orthodox, conservative, reform, and other sects of Judaism. Consult a rabbi of the sect of which the deceased was a member, for further information. There are many Jewish traditions that seem to be in conflict with a police funeral, such as omission of flowers, plain caskets with no handles (this is a complication for an honor guard), and the rush to bury the body, sometimes within 24 hours.

The Five Stages of Grief

The Kübler-Ross model, commonly known as the five stages of grief, was first introduced by Elisabeth Kübler-Ross in her 1969 book, *On Death and Dying*.

1. Denial—"I feel fine."; "This can't be happening, not to me." Denial is usually only a temporary defense for the individual. This feeling is generally replaced with heightened awareness of positions and individuals that will be left behind after death.

2. Anger—"Why me? It's not fair!"; "How can this happen to me?"; "Who is to blame?"   Once in the second stage, the individual recognizes that denial cannot continue.

    Because of anger, the person is very difficult to care for because of misplaced feelings of rage and envy. Any individual that symbolizes life or energy is subject to projected resentment and jealousy.

3. Bargaining—"Just let me live to see my children graduate."; "I'll do anything for a few more years."; "I will give my life savings if..."   The third stage involves the hope that the individual can somehow postpone or delay death. Usually, the negotiation for an extended life is made with a higher power in exchange for a reformed lifestyle. Psychologically, the individual is saying, "I understand I will die, but if I could just have more time..."

4. Depression—"I'm so sad, why bother with anything?"; "I'm going to die... What's the point?"; "I miss my loved one, why go on?"

    During the fourth stage, the dying person begins to understand the certainty of death. Because of this, the individual may become silent, refuse visitors and spend much of the time crying and grieving.

This process allows the dying person to disconnect oneself from things of love and affection. It is not recommended to attempt to cheer up an individual who is in this stage. It is an important time for grieving that must be processed.

5. Acceptance—"It's going to be okay."; "I can't fight it, I may as well prepare for it." In this last stage, the individual begins to come to terms with his mortality or that of his loved one.

The funeral helps the family progress through the grief stages. The pomp and circumstance of the police funeral allows the mourning of different persons – community members, partners, friends, and family. The police funeral allows for private moments, as well as public spectacle.

When one of our sentinels is murdered, it upsets our society's sense of order. The police keep us safe; when someone kills a police officer, this offends the society, and rips the fabric of our community.

How to Get Inexpensive Rifles, Handguns and Shotguns From the Federal Government

Sometimes the police department is short-sighted in its treatment of the honor guard. The honor guard is often poorly funded and ignored. Sometimes honor guards are not afforded training time, and work with poor or outdated equipment. This section will give resources to the police department. It is distasteful to say, but after a funeral is the best time to ask to update uniforms and equipment.

The Defense Logistics Agency (DLA) Disposition Services (formerly known as the Defense Reutilization and Marketing Service) maintains the DRMS Law Enforcement Support Office (LESO). There is a Project User Manual (UM) for getting unissued firearms from the military. These wonderful acronym-happy people will give you great surplus guns cheap.

Under Section 1033 of the National Defense Authorization Act for fiscal year 1997 (10 U.S.C.2576a) the Secretary of Defense may transfer to Federal and State agencies personal property of the Department of Defense, including weapons, that the Secretary determines is suitable for use by the agencies in law enforcement activities. Agencies in law enforcement activities are defined as government agencies whose primary function is the enforcement of applicable Federal, state and local laws, and whose law enforcement officers have powers of arrest and apprehension. All requests for weapons from State and local law enforcement agencies must be submitted through the appropriate governor- appointed state coordinator for approval.   The program will allow you to get thousand -dollar M16 rifles for $50! I know, this is incredible! Of course, these cannot be sold, traded, or donated once your agency gets them. These cannot be purchased for individuals either.

For those who like stats, the M16 Rifle is in caliber: 5.56 x 45mm (.223), and uses a gas, direct action mechanism, is selective fire, and uses a 20 or 30 round box magazine. These rifles are FULL AUTO. The rate of fire is 700-950 rounds per minute; they must be converted. The auto sears must be retained, since these rifles remain the property of the government. The weight is 6.30 lbs. (2.86kg) empty; the length is 39.00" (990mm). The muzzle velocity is 3,280ft/sec (1000m/sec), with an effective Range of 1312 ft (400m).

The M14 rifles are only $100! The caliber is 7.62x51mm NATO (.308 Win.) The Mechanism: Rotating bolt, gas operated, air cooled, semi-automatic magazine fed rifle. The Weight is 8.55 lbs. (3.88kg) empty. The length is 44.1" (112cm). The muzzle velocity is 2,800ft/sec (853m/sec).

The M1911 semiautomatic pistols can be had for $50. Most readers will be familiar with this .45 ACP caliber pistol. This is a short recoil, self-loading, pistol which uses a 7-round box magazine. The pistol is single action, so some departmental orders forbid this pistol. The weight is 2.4 lbs. (1.13kg). The length: 8.6" (219mm), with a barrel of 4.9" (127mm).

The LESO Application is accessed through the DRMS Web Site. The path to the application starts from the DRMS home page at http:www.drms.dla.mil. The user selects "I am a Military, Government, Nonprofit, or Public Service Agency (Reutilization, Transfer, Donation Customers)." This displays the starting R/T/D page. Along the left border under Reutilization heading is a choice for "LESO". Selecting "LESO" will take the user to the LESO application start page.

Effective June 2, 2010 Allocation limits have been adjusted to the following: M16 Rifles to 100%, M14 Rifle to 50%, 38 caliber and .45 caliber pistols to 100%, and Military Series Shotguns to 10%.

The Law Enforcement Support Office (LESO) is the point of contact for Law Enforcement Agencies (LEAs) to acquire Department of Defense (DOD) excess weapons through the 1033 program. There are some responsibilities that Law Enforcement Agencies (LEA's) have. LESO reminds LEAs that weapons obtained through the 1033 program are on loan from the DOD and remain the property of the DOD.

Trading, bartering or selling of the weapons is strictly prohibited by the Memorandums of Agreements signed between your state and LESO and your state and the U.S. Army Tank-Automotive and Armaments Command (TACOM).

Any incidents of trading, bartering, selling, damage to, or theft of 1033 Program weapons will be forwarded to the DLA Accountability office, which has special investigators, empowered with arrest and apprehension authority, for further investigation.

LEAs are responsible for acquiring magazines and slings to use with weapons acquired through the 1033 Program. Magazines/Clips and slings are not issued with the weapons. Florida agencies contact:

Rita Acevedo Surplus Property Supervisor
LESO and SASP Contact
Bureau of Federal Property Assistance
14281 U.S. Highway 301 South
Starke, Florida 32091
Phone: 904-964-5601
Fax: 904-964-4815
rita.acevedo@dms.myflorida.com

Agencies from other states can check the website:

http:www.drms.dla.mil.

LAW ENFORCEMENT AGENCY (LEA)
WEAPON REQUEST
INSTRUCTIONS

1. LEAs requesting weapons are required to have an up-to-date application on hand with the Law Enforcement Support Office

(LESO) with a point of contact for weapons listed. Without either of these items the processing of the request could be delayed.

2. This template is fillable. It is preferred that the request be typed rather than hand-written.

3. Fill out the agency information at the top of the template. This portion must be complete and include the Requesting Agency ID, name, address (P.O. Boxes are not accepted), and contact information. If the Agency ID is not known, contact the appropriate State Coordinator. Federal Agencies will need to contact the LESO directly for this information.

4. Enter the type and quantity of each weapon being requested. The type of weapons available and the allocation limit for each is available on the LESO website. Requests for weapons that are not available will be discarded without a response. Do not fill in the LESO USE ONLY area.

5. A justification is required for all requests. Do not use blanket statements (i.e. For Law Enforcement Use); be specific. When quantities are limited preference will be given to teams dealing with counterdrug / counterterrorism activities. Further justification may be requested by LESO.

6. The Chief Executive Official/Head of Agency – Local Field Office must initial each item indicating their understanding of the rules and regulations concerning 1033 weapons. The initials cannot be typed.

7. The Chief Executive Official/Head of Agency – Local Field Office must sign approving the request. The Chief Executive Official/Head of Local Agency is the only one who is able to sign approving the request unless LESO has a letter granting

signing authority to another individual. The letter must be signed by the Chief Executive Official/Head of Agency – Local Field Office and state that the person named has signing authority for the 1033 Program.

8. All requests must be approved and signed by the appropriate State Coordinator. Any request received that is not approved by the appropriate State Coordinator will be returned to the requestor. Federal Agencies do not have this requirement and send their requests directly to the LESO.

The Department of the Army
Ceremonial Rifle Program

By law, the M1 Garand is the only authorized rifle for this program. Up to 15 of these rifles will be sent to the agency requesting.

The issue of rifles at no cost is predicated upon an organization meeting the specific requirements of the law and policy that govern this program, along with the availability of funds. Law enforcement agencies usually have to reimburse the United States Government for any shipping costs. The current charge for this is approximately $50 per rifle.

Money for the ceremonial rifle program is not handled by the Army Static Display and Ceremonial Rifle Team located in Warren, Michigan. If an organization is required to pay for the shipment of rifles, the US Army TACOM Life Cycle Management Command in Rock Island, Illinois will inform the agency.

Storage of the ceremonial rifles is at the discretion of the organization. You are required to store the rifles in a safe, secure environment as directed by the gun laws within your state.

If an organization has rifles that are no longer required for any reason, i.e. Post/Detachment is closing, the honor guard is disbanded, etc., you must return them to Army control at your own expense. Your organization is NOT authorized to give away or transfer these weapons.

Contact:
http://www.tacom.army.mil/ceremonial_rifle/law-enforce.htm

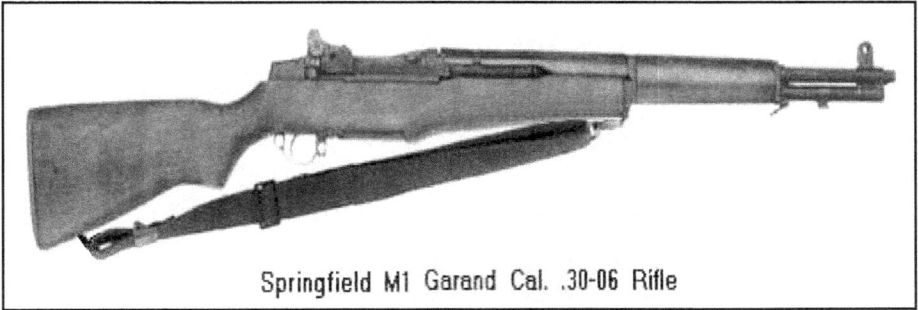

Springfield M1 Garand Cal. .30-06 Rifle

Helping the Family

The ultimate purpose of police policy is to establish procedures and guidelines to direct the department's administration to provide emotional care for a deceased officer's family through contingency plans and procedures.

The department has the responsibility to provide liaison assistance to the immediate survivors of an officer who dies in the line-of-duty. This responsibility provides tangible and intangible emotional support for the surviving family during this traumatic period of   readjustment.

A comprehensive list of survivors' benefits with clarification should be provided to the family as well as continued emotional support for the family.

Assisting the Family
at the Hospital

The first ranking officer to arrive at the hospital should become the hospital liaison. The hospital liaison officer should be in command during the arrival of immediate survivors, police officials, the press and others.

These responsibilities include: making arrangements with the hospital personnel for appropriate waiting facilities. There should be private areas reserved for immediate survivors, the Chief of Police, the Notification Officer, and others requested by the immediate survivors.

A separate room should be designated for fellow police officers and friends. The hospital liaison should request this from the hospital administrator.

A separate room should be designated for press staging area. The hospital liaison should request this from the hospital administrator.

The hospital liaison should ensure that medical personnel relate pertinent information of the officer's condition to the family first. The hospital liaison should request this from the doctor in charge of the deceased officer's care.

The hospital liaison should notify the appropriate hospital personnel that all billing for medical services shall be directed only to the police department. The family should not receive any of these bills at their residence address. This will require the hospital liaison to re-contact the hospital later during normal business hours to ensure proper billing takes place.

The notification officer should arrange transportation for the immediate survivors and others from the hospital back to their residence.

Do not be overly protective of the family. This includes the sharing of specific information on how the officer died, as well as allowing the family time with the deceased officer.

Idle promises such as "we'll promote him posthumously", or 'we'll retire her badge" should not be made to the family. Do not suggest a survivor be sedated unless medication is requested by that survivor.

Support for the Family
During Wake & Funeral

Within 24 hours of death, the Chief of Police should designate a funeral liaison officer, a benefits coordinator, a family support advocate, and a department liaison. These designations should be announced to the department in writing and all referrals are made according to the areas of responsibility.

The Chief of Police should personally notify the surviving family of the designated choices. The communications supervisor may require additional employees or overtime to field incoming phone calls. Callers should be directed to the appropriate liaison, according to the responsibility.

Within 24 hours the Chief of Police or appropriate designee should make appropriate referrals under an Employee Assistance Program for critical incident stress debriefing for officers close to the incident, and referrals for the surviving family if they wish.

Benefits Coordinator

The Chief of Police should designate a Lieutenant, Captain or Major to act as Benefits Coordinator.

This member should coordinate filing workman's compensation claims and related paperwork, gather information on all benefits or funeral payments available to the family, and field all phone calls and inquiries regarding the establishment of any trust funds or education funds.

There should be a clear distinction between benefits, (which are financial payments made to the family to ensure financial stability following the loss of a loved one) and funeral payments, (which are funds specifically earmarked for funeral expenses).

The Benefits Coordinator should prepare a printout or other documentation of the benefits/funeral payments due to the family, listing named beneficiaries, contacts at various benefits offices, and when they can expect to receive the benefit.

The Benefits Coordinator should file all benefit-related paperwork, and follow through with the family to ensure that these benefits are being received. Private consultants/attorneys should NOT be used for this purpose if they intend to bill the family for the services.

The Benefits Coordinator is a lifeline for the family. This member should visit with the surviving family within a few days following the funeral to discuss benefits. The prepared printout and other documentation should be made available to the family at that time.

If there are surviving children from a former marriage,

the guardian of those children should also receive a printout of what benefits the child will be receiving.   The Benefits Co-ordinator should pay special attention to problems regarding possible revocation of   health benefits. The vast majority of survivors are given a 30 day grace period before being can-celed from the coverage or being responsible for monthly pay-ments for the coverage.

The Benefits Coordinator should advise the family of the role of police associations and organizations such as the Fraternal order of Police in making their attorney or financial counselor   available to the surviving family for whatever legal or financial counseling is   necessary, such as estab-lishing trust funds or other financial instruments.

This attorney should not be   affiliated with the de-partment and should work as an avid advocate for the family's interest.

Family Support Advocate

The Family Support Advocate should act as a long-term liaison with the surviving family. The family support advocate should have extensive experience in dealing with police vic-tims and witnesses.

The Notification Officer or the Funeral Liaison Officer may also serve as Family Support Advocate. This officer should not be a principle witness in the criminal trial. This of-ficer's responsibilities include maintaining contact with the surviving family to keep them abreast of criminal   proceed-ings. The family should never learn of developments of the case from the press prior to learning them from the depart-ment.

The Family Support Advocate should accompany the family to any criminal proceedings, introduce them to prosecutors, and answer any questions they may have during the criminal trial.

This officer cooperates with outside peer support groups, and ensures that the surviving family does not feel totally isolated from the department.

The Advocate should encourage others to make visits or help with family needs of the surviving family. Care should be used that idle promises are not made to the surviving family. The Family Support Advocate should invite the surviving family to the Police Memorial Day ceremonies.

The management of the department must realize that the Family Support Advocate should not set time limitations on when the family should "recover" from this traumatic event. The grief process has no timetable. Survivors may experience a complicated grief process.

Survivors should continue to feel a part of the "police family" for which the officer gave his/her life. The Family Support Advocate should keep in touch with the family with monthly phone calls through the first year, dwindling off as necessary. The needs of the survivors usually dictate the frequency of contact.

The Advocate should ensure that the anniversary date of the officer's death is observed with a note to the family and/or flowers sent to the grave; and that adequate support is given to the family during holidays, particularly during the first year.

The Family Support Advocate should work with community groups and government leaders towards the establishment of any appropriate memorials, plaques or memorabilia, and considers surviving parents with any presentations. The surviving family should continue to receive support and invitations from the Chief of Police to appropriate department social activities.

Line of Duty
Death Benefits

The following is a list of benefits available to survivors of law enforcement officers killed in the line of duty; it is recommended that officers familiarize themselves with this list and give a copy to both family members and the family attorney.

The Federal Bureau of Justice Assistance, Office of Justice Programs, Public Safety Officers' Benefits Program offers death benefits for survivors. PSOB provides a one-time benefit to eligible survivors of public safety officers whose deaths were the direct and proximate result of an injury sustained in the line of duty on or after September 29, 1976. For the current death benefit amount, visit the PSOB web site at www.psob.gov.   PSOB also provides a one-time benefit to eligible public safety officers who were permanently and totally disabled, as a result of a catastrophic injury sustained in the line of duty, on or after November 29, 1990. Injuries must permanently prevent officers from performing any gainful work in the future. For the current disability benefit amount, visit www.psob.gov.

We must not forget that survivors who are wounded have feelings of survivor's guilt, inadequacy, and impotence.

PSOB provides support for higher education to eligible spouses and children of public safety officers who died in the line of duty on or after January 1, 1978, or were catastrophically disabled in the line of duty on or after October 3, 1996. For the current maximum educational assistance amount per month, visit www.psob.gov.

The following checklist is provided to streamline the PSOB filing process for the fallen officer's survivors. Call the PSOB Office for assistance with part of the PSOB claim.

The benefits coordinator must collect the information regarding the officer's line of duty death from agency records.

Among the records needed are the PSOB Report of Public Safety Officer's Death form, which must be completed and signed by the head of the police agency or designee, a detailed statement of circumstances from the initiation of the incident to the pronouncement of the officer's death, investigation, incident, and accident reports, if any, are required.

In addition, the death certificate, autopsy report, and toxicology report, or a statement signed by the head of the public safety agency or designee explaining that none were performed, all are necessary.

Collect the information regarding the officer's survivor's beneficiaries. E-mail fax, or mail the above information to the PSOB Office, and keep a complete copy for your records.

The PSOB Claim for Death Benefits form should be completed and signed by the survivor/ claimant. Obtain the officer's current marriage certificate, if applicable. Obtain divorce decrees for the officer's and current spouse's previous marriages, including references to physical custody of any children, if applicable.

Obtain death certificates for the officer's and current spouse's previous marriages, if any of the marriages ended in death, if applicable. Obtain birth certificates for all the officer's surviving children and step-children, regardless of age or dependency, identifying the children's parents, if applicable.

Contact Public Safety Officers' Benefits Office, Bureau of Justice Assistance, Office of Justice Programs, at 810 Seventh Street NW. Fourth Floor Washington, DC 20531 Phone: 202–307–0635 Toll-free: 1–888–744–6513 E-mail: AskPSOB@usdoj.gov PSOB web site: www.psob.gov

Law Enforcement Officers who are NRA members, killed in the line of duty, will have $25,000 in life insurance coverage. E-mail membership@nrahq.org. or contact the NRA via mail at the following address: National Rifle Association of America, 11250 Waples Mill Road, Fairfax, VA 22030. Contact the NRA via phone at: NRA Member Programs, 1-800-672-3888.

The PBA or FOP offers a cash donation to families of PBA or FOP members killed in the line of duty. For more information contact The Police Benevolent Association or Fraternal Order of Police.

The county or department may provide certain death and pension benefits pursuant to the applicable FOP or PBA contract and the Employee Manual.

The state may pay benefits as well. The State of Florida pursuant to F.S. 112.19 pays to the beneficiary designated by officer during life and delivered by state. Other states may offer like benefits. Florida pays $59,694.46 if death is accidental, $59,694.46 if death is accidental and officer was in "fresh pursuit" or responding to an emergency, or $179,083.29 if unlawfully and intentionally killed.

The State of Florida pursuant to F.S. 112.193 provides that upon the death of law enforcement officer, the employer may present to the spouse or other beneficiary of the officer, upon request, one complete uniform, including the badge worn by the officer.

However, if the law enforcement officer is killed in the line of duty, the employer may present, upon request, to the spouse or other beneficiary of the officer, the officer's service-issued handgun, if one was issued as part of the officer's equipment.

If the employer is not in possession of the service-issued handgun, the employer may, within its discretion, and upon written request of the spouse or other beneficiary, present a similar handgun.

The State of Florida pursuant to F.S.440.16 pays compensation for death, if death results from the accident within 1 year thereafter or follows continuous disability and results from the accident within 5 years thereafter, the employer shall pay: (a) Within 14 days after receiving the bill, actual funeral expenses not to exceed $7,500.

The State of Florida pursuant to F.S.440.16 (b), pays

compensation, in addition to the above, but such compensation shall be subject to the limits provided in s. 440.12(2), and shall not exceed $150,000. All dependents or persons entitled to compensation, 66 2/3 percent of the average wage to the spouse, if there is no child, 50 percent of the average weekly wage, such compensation to cease upon the spouse's death.

Contact the Division of Workers Compensation: Division of Workers' Compensation Assessments Unit, 200 East Gaines Street, Tallahassee, FL 32399-4221, (800) 219-8953

The State of Florida pursuant to F.S. 112.19 2(3) states that if a law enforcement officer is accidentally killed or unlawfully and intentionally killed the state shall waive certain educational expenses that the child or spouse of the deceased officer incurs while obtaining a career certificate, an undergraduate education, or a postgraduate education.

The amount waived by the state shall be an amount equal to the cost of tuition and matriculation and registration fees for a total of 120 credit hours. The child or spouse may attend a state career center, a state community college, or a state university. The child or spouse may attend any or all of the institutions specified in this subsection, on either a full-time or part-time basis.

The benefits provided to a child under this subsection shall continue until the child's 25th birthday. The benefits provided to a spouse under this subsection must commence within 5 years after the death occurs, and entitlement thereto shall continue until the 10th anniversary of that death. The waiver can be obtained from the registrar of the school the child attends.

The State of Florida pursuant to F.S. 440.16 (c) pays to the surviving spouse, payment of postsecondary student fees for instruction at any career center up to 1,800 classroom hours or payment of student fees at any community college established under part III of chapter 1004 for up to 80 semester hours. The spouse of a deceased state employee shall be entitled to a full waiver of such fees. The benefits provided for in this paragraph shall be in addition to other benefits provided for in this section and shall terminate 7 years after the death of the deceased employee, or when the total payment in eligible compensation under paragraph (b) has been received.

The State of Florida pursuant to F.S. 112.19(h)1 provides that any employer who employs a full-time law enforcement officer who suffers a catastrophic injury, in the line of duty shall pay the entire premium of the employer's health insurance plan for the injured employee, the injured employee's spouse, and for each dependent child of the injured employee until the child reaches the age of majority or until the end of the calendar year in which the child reaches the age of 25.

There exists a "Dignity Memorial Funeral, Cremation and Cemetery Providers created the Public Servants Program", for emergency service personnel. This program provides dignified and honorable tributes, at no cost, for career and volunteer law enforcement officers who fall in the line of duty. Visit their website for complete information at www.dignitymemorial.com and look under Public Servants for details. Call 800-344-6489.

Death within 90 Days of Retirement

There is a provision in federal agencies that should be adopted by every police department in the nation. In the event a sworn police department law enforcement officer dies within 90 days after taking retirement, the retirement should re-age so that the date of retirement shall be shown as the day of death, so as to afford any and all benefits possible to the family of the officer.

Concerns of Police Survivors, Inc.

COPS is a national, non-profit organization that works with law enforcement agencies, police organizations, mental health professionals, and local peer-support organizations to provide assistance to surviving families of law enforcement officers killed in the line of duty. COPS has become a "lifeline" to police survivors nationwide. Contact the COPS National Office at

www.nationalcops.org/chap.htm
or at
P.O. Box 3199
3096 S. State Highway 5
Camdenton, MO 65020
Phone: 573-346-4911
Fax: 573-346-1414

The TASER Foundation
Supporting the Family

According to TASER Foundation (2011), the foundation distributes financial gifts to the families of fallen officers in the U.S. and Canada through donations and an initial endowment of $1,000,000 that was created by TASER International and the direct contributions from TASER International employees. Grants are available only upon request by the chiefs of police and sheriffs as well as federal law enforcement executives in the name of officers killed in the line of duty since August 1, 2004 going forward.

TASER International, Inc. bears all of the administrative costs of the TASER Foundation in order to ensure 100 percent of all donations are distributed to the families of fallen officers. The TASER Foundation is a 501(c)3 tax exempt corporation. All donations are tax deductible to the extent allowable by law.

To protect and serve - every day over 850,000 law enforcement officers in the United States and Canada work to fulfill this mission. Sometimes these officers make the ultimate sacrifice and are tragically killed in the line of duty.

In 2004, 153 officers in the United States and 7 in Canada were tragically killed in the line of duty. Over 6,000 law enforcement agencies have lost officers in the line of duty. The average age of an officer lost in the line of duty is only 38 years old.

In response to these tragedies, and as a way to give back to the law enforcement community, TASER® International, Inc. established the TASER Foundation in November 2004. The initial endowment of $1,000,000 came from TASER International, Inc. and the direct contributions from TASER International employees.

As of December 31, 2004 the TASER Foundation has awarded $188,500 to the families of fallen law enforcement officers in the United States and Canada. Please donate to this worthy cause. Visit their website at: www.taser.com.

The Honor Guard has a special opportunity to make a multi-year commitment to the families of fallen officers.

Watch Society: $1,000 per year for four years (Co-sponsor a family)

Shield Society: $2,500 per year for four years (Sponsor one family per year)

Sentry Society: $5,000 per year for four years (Sponsor two families per year)

Legacy Society: $50,000 one time gift (endowment gift to perpetually provide one grant per year)

Funeral Administration

The department may have little time to organize an event of the magnitude of a police funeral. One might think of a police funeral like a Broadway show. There are many things to consider. There is lighting, food, water, equipment, and vehicles. There are animals and people. There is news and television media.

Police funerals can draw thousands of people, giant motorcades of motorcycles and police cars, and the media. A funeral may be delayed due to autopsy, or rushed due to family concerns (some religions mandate that the body be buried as soon as possible, some within 48 hours.)

Advance preparation is crucial. Departments must arrange advance preparations and funding, and keep in mind that multiple officers killed in a single event, increasing the costs and complexity.

Definitions:

Benefits Coordinator: The officer designated by the Chief of Police responsible to act as coordinator for benefits for the family. It is a distinct honor and grave responsibility to be chosen for this detail.

Department Liaison: The officer designated by the Chief of Police is responsible for making expedient provisions for all department resources and delegation of tasks, and will direct the funeral activities of the department and visiting police agencies, according to the wishes of the family. It is a distinct honor and grave responsibility to be chosen for this detail.

Family Support Advocate: The officer designated by the

Chief of Police responsible to act as a long-term liaison with the surviving family. It is a distinct honor and grave responsibility to be chosen for this detail.

Funeral Liaison Officer: The officer designated by the Chief of Police **is** responsible for acting as a facilitator between the decedent's family and the department during the wake and funeral. It is a distinct honor and grave responsibility to be chosen for this detail.

Great Bodily Harm/Serious Physical Injury: Bodily injuries serious enough to either create a substantial risk of death; permanent disability/disfigurement; or long-term loss/impairment of the functioning of any bodily member or organ.

Honor Guard Commander: The honor guard commander is a sergeant who is an expert in funerary ceremony. This commander should have attended the Broward County Honor Guard Academy at least once. It is a distinct honor and grave responsibility to be chosen for this detail.

Hospital Liaison: The officer designated as the first ranking officer to arrive at the hospital, becomes responsible and in command during the arrival of immediate survivors, police officials, the press and others, and is liaison between the department and the hospital.

Line-Of-Duty Death: Any action felonious or accidental (automobile accidents, training accidents etc.), which claims the life of a law enforcement officer who was performing police functions while on or off duty. The Chief of Police may put certain parts of this directive into effect for cases of natural death of an officer.

Notification Officer: The officer designated by the Chief of

Police, who is responsible for ensuring that timely notification is made to the surviving family.

Survivors: Include immediate family members of the deceased officer, spouse, children, parents, siblings, fiancée and/or significant other.

Death Notification

A proper procedure must be followed in case of critically injured officers with poor prognosis or obvious line-of-duty death.

Timeliness takes precedence over protocol in the death notification process. The senior ranking officer on the scene is generally responsible for ensuring that timely notification is made to the surviving family. Upon confirmation of death, a death notification must be made to the immediate survivors shortly after or coinciding with normal command notifications.

It is so important to notify the family in person, before they find out from email, cell phones, or news media, that the importance cannot be overstated.

The Chief of Police should designate a ranking officer as notification officer. The Chief may assign at least one other officer or personally accompany the notification officer, if circumstances permit.

If the Chief of Police or appropriate division commander is not immediately available to make this designation, responsibility for designating a notification officer remains with the senior ranking officer. In no instance should the staff officer making notification be of a rank of less than lieutenant; notifications should never be made alone.

Notification must always be made in person. The Police Chaplain and Chief of Police (or designee) should accompany the informing officer whenever possible. If a Police Chaplain is not available, then a Police Chaplain from a neighboring department should be sought out. If these persons are not readily accessible, notification should not be delayed.

The surviving family should hear of the death from a department representative first and not from the press, media or other source. Using emergency lights is permissible in this circumstance, but the speed limit should not be exceeded.

If the opportunity to transport the family to the hospital prior to the death of the officer presents itself, then the family should be transported without waiting for the appropriate staff to gather. After the death of the officer, if the family wants to go to the hospital they should be transported via police vehicle.

Using emergency lights is permissible in this circumstance, but the speed limit should not be exceeded. It is highly recommended that the family not drive themselves to the hospital. Should there be a serious resistance, and the family insists on driving, an officer should accompany them in the family vehicle.

The notification officer should be aware that as soon as the family sees the notification group they will know something is wrong. Ask to be admitted into the house.

Never make a death notification on the doorstep. Gather everyone in the home and ask them to sit down, inform them slowly and clearly of the information you have on the incident, making sure you use the officer's name during the notification.

If the officer has already died, the notification officer shall relay that information using words like "died" and "dead" rather than "gone away" and "passed on", which spark a false sense of hope.

The notification officer will be seriously affected by the death; showing emotions is perfectly acceptable. Reactions of the family may include hysteria, anger, fainting, physical violence, or shock.

Officers and dispatchers should be aware that in the

event of an on-duty-death, the news media will be monitoring the police frequency. Communications regarding particulars of the notifications should be restricted to the telephone rather than the radio whenever possible.

The name of the deceased officer must never be provided to the media before the immediate survivors living in the region are notified. If the media already has the officer's name, a staff officer should request they withhold this information, pending notification of the next of kin.

Any notification of immediate survivors beyond the county in which the officer serves should be made through personal death notification by the local law enforcement agency in that area. The notification officer should obtain the names of relatives to contact from the immediate survivor.

The notification officer should contact that jurisdiction personally by telephone. If no contact by phone is possible, the notification officer should pass this information to a Communications Supervisor who should ensure a teletype message is sent to that jurisdiction, requesting personal death notification.

Department Liaison

This position should be filled by a lieutenant, captain or major because of the need to make expedient provisions of all department resources and delegation of tasks, and should be chosen by the Chief of Police.

The department liaison will work closely with the funeral liaison officer to ensure the needs and request of the family are fulfilled regarding funeral arrangements.

The department liaison directs the funeral activities of the department and visiting police agencies, according to the wishes of the family. The department liaison is also responsible for oversight of arrangements for travel, lodging, and airport shuttle for out-of-town family members.

The department liaison should conduct a survey of alternate churches and reception halls with seating large enough to accommodate a law enforcement funeral. This information will be passed on to the family as soon as possible to assist the family in making a decision on a location. The choice remains with the family.

The department liaison should coordinate all official law enforcement communications and arrangements for a law enforcement funeral, including honor guards, pall bearers, traffic control and liaise with all visiting law enforcement agencies.

The department liaison should liaise with media rather than the PIO; the PIO will not be able to take on this task because of other responsibilities. In the unlikely event that the family should decide to accept an interview, an officer should attend and "screen" all questions being presented to the family, so as not to jeopardize upcoming legal proceedings. The PIO will give specific instructions on what information may be released.

The department liaison should arrange for routine residence checks of the survivor's home for 6-8 weeks following the death. This service is necessary since the survivors may be spending much time away from the home with legal matters. This may require outside liaison with other jurisdictions

Funeral Liaison Officer

The funeral liaison officer may be an officer, detective, or sergeant, and should be chosen by the Chief of Police.

The Funeral Liaison Officer should act as a facilitator between the decedent's family and the department during the wake and funeral. The position requires the officer have good knowledge of the family relationships, but not be so emotionally involved with the loss, that he/she would become ineffective.

The Liaison Officer is responsible for meeting with the

family and explaining the responsibilities of a funeral liaison officer, including being constantly available to the family throughout the wake and funeral, and ensuring that the needs of the family come before the wishes of the department.

The Funeral Liaison Officer is responsible for meeting with the family and funeral director regarding funeral arrangements. Since most officers have not pre-arranged their wishes for the handling of their own funeral, the family will need to decide all aspects of the funeral. The funeral liaison officer should only make the family aware of what the department may offer in the way of assistance and resources.

The Liaison Officer is responsible for relaying all available information to the surviving family concerning the circumstances of death and any continuing investigation. Police departments traditionally withhold this type of information, particularly in sensitive homicide cases. The funeral liaison officer should coordinate with investigating officers and prosecutors to ensure that the family receives as much information as possibly allowable during the first few days. "Not being kept informed" is a common complaint of surviving families.

The Liaison Officer is responsible for determining the need for travel arrangements for out-of-town family members or any other special needs during the funeral, and reporting to the department liaison.

The Funeral Liaison Officer is responsible for briefing the family on law enforcement funeral procedures such as the 21 gun salute, playing of "Taps", drum and bag pipe corps, and presentation of flag.

Covering of Police Badge

The covering of the police badge is a mark of respect for officers who have died in the line of duty, and is appropriate in those cases where an officer has been killed in the line of duty or has died while on duty. The police badge will be covered for any police officer killed in the line of duty or who dies while on duty. The mourning band is to be worn from the time of death to the conclusion of police honors.

For other law enforcement officers serving neighboring counties who are killed in the line of duty, the mourning band is to be worn from the time of death to the conclusion of police honors.

For any memorial service honoring law enforcement officers killed in the line of duty, the mourning band is to be worn during the duration of the service.

The Police Monument shall be draped in black material approximating a mourning band, on the anniversary of the end of watch. An appropriate ceremony shall be observed, and the US flag shall be flown at half-mast for a twenty-four hour period. This ceremony shall be observed for the death of any police officer, and on the anniversary of that death. The Mourning band is to be draped from the time of death to the conclusion of police honors.

Ceremonial Guidelines

The following are the guidelines developed to assist in the Ceremonial preparations common for law enforcement funeral procedure. Guidelines are just that; not rules and not commands.

There will always be those that are shocked and disappointed if what they see is not what they experienced "in the Marines" or "in the Army". Police are not military. Police are not firefighters. A department may have traditions or styles that are not familiar to everyone. The guidelines include a respectful ceremonial aspect to everything. It doesn't have to be perfect; it just has to look perfect. The family and friends may not remember every detail, but they will be left with an impression of perfection that will last forever.

All department members are always strongly encouraged to proudly display their uniform while in attendance at all formal ceremonies, even if not currently in a uniform assignment. All personnel attending such ceremonies in uniform should wear formal Class A issued attire, with long sleeves and tie, unless otherwise authorized by the Chief of Police. The members should present a neatly groomed appearance.

Members who suffer a line-of-duty death should be posthumously awarded a "Medal of Valor" or other type of award in reverence for their service. This award should be presented during the funeral ceremony to the decedents immediate survivor; however if circumstances prevent this, then the award should be presented at a future appropriate police memorial service.

Law enforcement honors are intended for the decedent's family as well as the extended law enforcement family. Law enforcement honors are also intended to demonstrate to the family and community the high esteem in which the decedent officer is held by his agency and profession.

It is important that this intent be conveyed to the decedent's survivors by the funeral liaison officer and family support advocate, understanding that the ultimate decisions concerning various ceremonial aspects remain with the family.

An initial "support team" meeting should be scheduled the day following the death to bring all key individuals together to review progress to that point, communication needs, and coordinate plans. At least one other coordination meeting should be scheduled prior to the funeral or memorial ceremonies to confirm progress and identify any shortcomings.

As soon as the funeral arrangements have been made by the family through the funeral director, it is paramount that these be communicated by the agency by the funeral liaison officer to maximize planning time.

It should be the responsibility of the communications supervisor to insure that all notification of arrangements to other agencies be accomplished in a timely manner for planning purposes, and be updated as needed with more specific information as such develops.

Teletype will be used for outside agency updates, noting capabilities of fax machines to send detailed messages such as memorial notices, with instructions for outside agency participation and relevant maps.

The PIO should be responsible for all public notifications as well as the development of a "memorial notice". This is a single page description of the decedent's employment summary, or other relevant activities or accomplishments, birth history and family survivors, services information regarding wake and funeral information. This should be an attractively computer-designed product with a photograph, preferably one that can be photocopied for mass distribution.

Much of the same personal and professional history, along with a short line-of-duty death description should comprise an award certificate/letter noting the decedent being awarded the Department's "Medal of Valor". The PIO should draft this for the chief's signature, to be presented with the actual medal to the appropriate survivor at the funeral/memorial.

Roll call briefings should continuously update departmental personnel on developments, and facilitate an exchange of information. All departmental personnel are encouraged to attend roll call briefings during this period. The ceremonial briefing given to all attending departmental personnel in the hours just prior to the funeral or memorial service, will involve a large number of attendees and should therefore be scheduled in a large room and may necessitate use of the Commission Chambers.

Wake or Viewing

The Honor Guard should be posted throughout viewing periods. A casket guard or guards should be posted. These guards stand at attention in a pose called "reverent arms". This casket guard may be armed with a shotgun or M1 Garand.

The Honor Guard Commander should be consulted as an expert in funerary ceremony. This commander should be at least a sergeant and have attended the Broward County Honor Guard Academy at least once.

Motor officers should handle any desired escorts. Additional motor officers should be culled from area police departments. Coordination of the motor officers should be made via the patrol lieutenant.

Pallbearers should be selected by the family no later than this point, and these individuals should survey the site of the memorial and funeral service prior to the last viewing.

The department should work closely with representatives from these locations to plan the logistics of escorting the casket. During this same time frame, appointed ushers, Honor Guard supervisor(s) and individual site supervisor(s) should also survey the selected sites for planning respective responsibilities.

These responsibilities include parking, staging, seating, and ceremonial formations. Preparing diagramed plans may be helpful. Sufficient personnel should also be appointed to ensure effective implementation of these plans when they occur.

A pair of boots owned and worn by the deceased officer or a formal hat should be obtained from the family by the funeral liaison officer, for display in a military style. If these cannot be obtained, a pair of boots should be obtained from a vendor.

Funeral and memorial processions are important to the community and the family. Depending on the various religious beliefs and personal wishes of the decedent's family, a church, cemetery, or hall may or may not be utilized for a ceremony.

Funerals range from a full funeral including burial, to a memorial service only. At least one procession will be involved for any ceremony, starting with the removal of the decedent from the funeral home.

A police motorcade should accompany all processions, with motorcycles encouraged to handle any and all traffic posts so as the department personnel can remain as part of the procession. Department marked units should follow immediately behind the motorcade, hearse and family vehicles.

Unmarked vehicles will then be placed after marked units to conclude the procession.

It is encouraged that a drive-by the Police Department Headquarters be included in the route. This can be conducted with all vehicles appropriately staged at pre-determined locations in front of the station, with all lights activated and all personnel lined up between their vehicles at the position of "attention" prior to the arrival of the motorcade.

All on-duty department personnel working within the station, unless staffing a critical function, should be authorized to also line up to pay final respects to the decedent and his/her family. Arrangements should be made to switch all calls to the neighboring city for a minimum period of time to facilitate this. This can be coordinated by a major, deputy chief, or assistant chief.

Six or eight honor guard members shall bear the pall, as appropriate. Heavier officers may require eight. A detail commander is assigned to command the pall bearers.

During the service, the Casket Guard should be changed every 15 minutes. The replacement guard will march slowly to the casket, salute, and relieve the guard. The Casket Guard will then come to "reverent arms". Four M1 rifles or shotguns are normally used by the Casket Guard.

On top of the casket there are normally four items: the American Flag, the formal hat or headgear of the officer, the badge, and the decorations that officer earned throughout his career.

The honor guard members will, at the conclusion of the remarks, and prior to burial, approach the coffin. One honor guard member will be at the head, and one at the foot. The member at the head will gather the badge, decorations, and hat from the casket, and give them to a third honor guard member.

The chief of police, mayor, and city manager act as dignitaries and usually do not participate, except to eulogize the dead, if desired.

When a cemetery is involved, where large numbers of attendees proceed from a separate location such as a church or hall and have to re-stage at a grave site, a "stalling tactic" for the family procession is important to allow time for this staging without the grieving family having to wait in their vehicles for an extended time period.

A small motorcade escorting the hearse and the family through an additional route that may be significant or symbolic to the decedent is further recommended.

Memorial Services

The following are traditional elements for a law enforcement funeral ceremony. These can take place in varied sequence, at varied locations, and may or may not be inclusive depending on the final wishes of the family.

The funeral liaison officer will insure that a notice is prepared prior to the   ceremony, noting the sequence of ceremonial events approved by the family,   for distribution to personnel prior to the ceremony.

A riderless black horse with formal boots turned backwards is led by a member of the mounted patrol. This detail is obtained from a neighboring department or Sheriff's office by the department liaison.

At the time of the flag folding, the members at the head and foot will take up the flag by the corners, and raise it about a foot to two feet above the casket. They will then sidestep so that they are now in front of the casket. The members then fold the flag lengthwise in fourths, so that the union now shows all around. Then the flag is then folded into a triangle, with the union showing all around, to symbolize the tricorn hats worn by our patriot forefathers.

The member will then present the flag to the Chief of Police, who will present it to the chief mourner, the wife or husband of the fallen, or the mother, if the fallen officer is un-married, or the oldest child if the officer has predeceased the spouse and there is no mother in attendance.

The Chief then says words to the effect of "On behalf of a grateful nation, community, and department, we present you this flag, with our condolences." An Honor Guard member then presents the badge, commendations, and headgear to the chief mourner. The casket is never lowered into the ground with these items or the flag.

A radio message should be utilized at the gravesite. A message to the unit may be used. In this case, we will use Lake Erika 407. "Attention all units: Lake Erika 407. Lake Erika 407. Lake Erika 407. Lake Erika 407 is now out of ser-vice". The attempted raising of the unit three times is a tech-nique that reminds all personnel of the day that officer could no longer respond to the radio call.

A separate police radio channel should be utilized for ceremonial coordination   (i.e. timing of the flyover, funeral liaison officer dispatch of "attention all units message", etc.), to avoid such communications being audible during the cere-mony while awaiting the "attention all units message".

Post Ceremony

A post ceremonial debriefing meeting should be sched-uled within one week after the funeral with all individuals in-volved in the planning of various activities in attendance. The primary purpose is to critique what went well and what could be improved upon, insure continued response as outlined in this policy, and assist the below remaining communications.

As it is difficult to identify all agencies represented at the various ceremonies, the police department does not wish to offend any agency through omission. An "all agencies teletype" message should be prepared by the communications supervisor and sent with the approval of the Chief of Police, generically thanking all agencies who "participated, extended their condolences, and offered their support".

Letters of appreciation from the department should be prepared by a major in a timely manner, for the chief's signature. These letters should be sent to those individuals and organizations who provided special assistance to the decedent's family, or the departments efforts while preparing the ceremonies and/or dealing with the loss of the decedent.

A department memorandum should be prepared and disseminated from the chief to all personnel, offering a message of appreciation for the professionalism of all members involved in the various activities, during a period of such professional and personal loss and grief, and, offering a healing message of encouragement.

A performance recognition or commendation should be prepared by the major, deputy chief, or assistant chief for the Chief of Police to issue, commending the notification officer, department liaison, hospital liaison, funeral liaison officer, benefits coordinator, honor guard commander, honor guard, motor officers, and any other member who made a significant contribution to the management of this detail.

When preparing the annual budget, the department should budget sufficient funds to prepare, plan, and execute a police funeral in the manner proscribed above. The department should review these plans as necessary to ensure that the department is ready in case of a line of duty death. A police funeral my run into tens of thousands of dollars. If multiple officers or a service animal are killed, representatives may attend from all over the state and other locations throughout the USA and even Canada.

Sample Officer's

Wishes Form

Name: _____

Date:_____

Update:_____	**Update:**_____
Update:_____	**Update:**_____
Update:_____	**Update:**_____
Update:_____	**Update:**_____

ORGAN DONATION

☐ I do not want any of my organs donated.

☐ I would like to have organs donated for transplant.

I would like to donate the following organs for transplant/research:

_____

FUNERAL DETAILS

Church Preference: _____

Religious Affiliation: _____

Clergyman: _____

Phone: _____

Funeral Home to be used: _____

Phone: _____

I have a pre-paid burial plan. Yes ☐ No ☐

Contact: _____

Service to be held at:

Funeral Home _____

 Name of Funeral Home: _____

Church _____

Name of Church: _____

I prefer:

Interment ☐ Entombment ☐ Cremation ☐

My choice of cemetery is: _____

☐ I have purchased a lot. ☐ I have not purchased a lot.

Lot is in name of: _____

Section _____

Lot _____

Block _____

Location of deed for lot: _____

If interment is in another city, give information on the receiving funeral home:

Name: _____

Phone: _____

Address: _____

Pallbearers:

_____

_____

_____

_____

_____

he Attorney who handled my will is

_____

at the law firm of _____

Phone number: _____

My last will is dated: _____

The Executor is: _____

POLICE FUNERALS

Social Security Number: _____

Date of Birth: _____

In case of death or serious injury, have a department representative contact:

Spouse: _____

Mother: _____

Father: _____

Close Relative: _____

Close Relative: _____

Close Relative: _____

Former Spouse (s): _____

My best friend on the department is

_____
and I would like him (her) to accompany anyone sent to give injury/death notice to my family. My best friend's address is:

_____

Phone number _____

The following members of my family have health concerns that the department should be aware of:

_____
_____

My family is aware of the beneficiaries listed on all my department insurance forms.

Yes ☐ No ☐

I have a letter written to my family explaining why I have named certain beneficiaries on my policies. Yes ☐ No ☐

I would like full law enforcement honors if killed in the line of duty. Yes ☐ No ☐

☐

Suggested departmental pallbearers:

_____
_____
_____

☐☐ Or standard honor guard pallbearers.

PERSONAL DOCUMENTS/INFORMATION

My birth date is: _____

My birth certificate is located at:

_____

I was born in: _____

My social security number: _____

Marriage 1:

I was married in: _____

On: _____

To: _____

Children from this marriage: _____

Children from this marriage: _____

I was divorced on: _____

State of: _____

If cremated, what do you wish done with your ashes?

_____

_____

Obituary: Yes ☐ No ☐

Please list the following in my obituary:

_____
_____
_____
_____

I am entitled to Veterans Benefits: Yes ☐ No ☐

I am entitled to Military Honors: Yes ☐ No ☐
☐ Army ☐ Navy ☐ USAF ☐ Marines ☐ USCG ☐ _____

I would like a "Lodge" service (available only to Master Masons): Yes ☐ No ☐

By: Lodge Number: _____ Worshipful Master: _____

☐ York Rite ☐ Scottish Rite ☐ Mahi Shrine ☐ Past Master ☐ Past DDGM

Flowers: Yes ☐ No ☐

Disposal of flowers: _____

Donations in lieu of flowers to:

_____

Musical selections:

_____
_____
_____

Special requests for service:

_____
_____
_____

SPECIAL FINAL REQUESTS

Special final requests should be addressed in one's will so your wishes will be upheld by a court of law. If you have not addressed these special final requests in a will, your primary beneficiary will have total control of your assets/possessions for final disposal. We strongly recommend addressing these issues in your will. If you choose not to, however, complete this section to alleviate your family of the decisions that might need to be made in your behalf.

This is how I would like insurance settlement money to be spent:

_____
_____
_____

This is how I would like real estate to be handled:

_____
_____
_____
_____
_____
_____

MY LIVING WILL

Individuals may execute a "living will" that instructs family members and physicians not to take extraordinary steps to continue your life on life-support machines. You should investigate the legality of the "living will" within your state, and take steps to execute the "living will" if you do not chose to be kept alive through mechanical means.

☐ I have not executed a "living will"

☐ I have executed a "living will"

Since copies of living wills may not be acceptable in some states, an *original, signed*

copy of my living will is readily accessible at:

_____

☐ Additional copies of my "living will" are on file with my personal physician, attorney, and with my will.

MY WILL

Your will should address special requests on how you would like insurance money to be spent, who you would like to have your prized possessions, etc. By providing this information in a will, your wishes can be upheld in court. Otherwise, your primary beneficiary will have total control of your assets/possessions. However, if this information is not included in your will, there is a section in this handbook for that information to be provided.

I do not have a will. ☐ (Oftentimes families incur additional emotional, legal and financial burdens when a loved one dies without having executed a will.

I have a will that is located at: _____

Marriage 2:

I was married in: _____

On: _____

To: _____

Children from this marriage: _____

Children from this marriage: _____

I was divorced on: _____

State of: _____

Marriage 3:

I was married in: _____

On: _____

To: _____

Children from this marriage: _____

Children from this marriage: _____

I was divorced on: _____

State of: _____

Current Marriage certificate (s) are located at:
_____

Divorce decree (s) are located at: _____

Children's birth certificates are located at:
_____

Children's adoption papers are located at:
_____

I served in the Armed Forces: Branch:

_____

Service Serial Number: _____

Enlisted on: _____

At: _____

Discharge Date: _____

Discharge papers located at: _____

Make a Logo For
Your Unit

If your department allows, why not make a logo for your unit? This logo can be used for tee shirts, magnetic signs for the van, or a decal for the patrol car. There are some things that are common to honor guard logos: rifles, swords, eagles, and wreaths. It is easy to make a logo. Doing an internet search can show you some nice logos. http://www.honorguardinc.com/ is a good place to look for anything honor guard-related. One might notice the logo – it is simple, elegant, and tasteful.

Design a logo and vote on it - then get some nice tee shirts made. After all, the honor guard is an elite unit, and should have a nice shirt.

I have included some samples for ideas. These logos may be used and adapted.

LAKE ERIKA

HONOR GUARD

Sample Badges

Hat Badges

HONOR GUARD
SERGEANT

Belt Buckle

Pins

FLAG TEAM

RIFLE TEAM

Training

There is an excellent training class available for those in the honor guard who wish to increase their skills and level of training. This class is 32 hours in length and a certificate is granted at the end. I have attended the academy twice. If interested, here is the information:

Honor Guard Academy
Practices & Protocols

Description: Emphasis on many Honor Guard components such as:

Casket Bearing
Casket Guard
Changing of Guard
Drill and Ceremony
Flag Carrying
Flag Folding
Funeral Protocol
Manual of Arms
Marching
Volley Rifle Salute

Facilitator: Police Honor Guard of Broward County Inc.

Fees: $50.00 Per Officer. This includes a shirt. (Make checks payable to: Police Honor Guard of Broward Co. Inc.)

Attendance: Attendance at the initial class session is mandatory. Uniform pants, hat and shoes required for class. The last day will be a mock funeral. Full honor guard uniform required.

Registration:

Submit registration form to:
Police HGA
P.O. Box 813552
Hollywood, Fl 33081-3552

This class is available for certified police, law enforcement, and fire personnel only. Class size limited to 100 students.

To get further information, go to the website at http://honorguardinc.com. Click on the download form link for registration form.

For more information:
Broward County Police Memorial Association (B.P.M.A.)
P.O. Box 813552
Hollywood, Florida 33081-3552
E-mail them at:
info@honorguardinc.com

For Further Reading

http://www.arlingtoncemetery.net/Taps .htm

http://www.west-point.org/Taps /Taps .html

http://www.nleomf.com/

http://www.ceremonialbugle.com/Products.htm

http://Tapsbugler.com/

http://honorguardinc.com/

Posted on POAT.org:

To Our Law Enforcement Family ~

Regrettably, it is with the utmost sadness that we have to send this notification. The Miami-Dade Police Department has suffered a great loss of two of our finest officers, Roger Castillo and Amanda Haworth, who were killed while serving a warrant in Miami-Dade County, Florida, on Thursday, January 20, 2011.

We will never forget the endeavor to which they dedicated their lives ~ serving the citizens of Miami-Dade County.

We will continue to stand united as a department, as co-workers, as friends, but most of all, as family. It is not in vain that this brave man and woman gave their lives. We will go on serving and protecting, as it is our duty to do so, and we will continue to uphold the law, as they would expect and want it to be.

We humbly ask for your continued thoughts and prayers for the Castillo and Haworth families.

The Police Officer Assistance Trust was founded in 1989 as a nonprofit support organization for the law enforcement community of Miami-Dade County, Florida. Our mission is to provide assistance to officers and their families in times of hardship, personal crisis, or critical need.

There was no resource or organization in place to assist officers who were facing devastating situations until POAT was formed. Since its inception, POAT has helped law enforcement families through catastrophic circumstances brought about by accident, illness, or injury. Assistance is primarily financial, but has extended to other support including information, referrals, and counseling.

To donate, checks should be made payable to the Police Officer Assistance Trust or POAT. Please notate Officers Castillo/Haworth Trust Fund in the memo area of your check.

Mail to:
Police Officer Assistance Trust
1030 NW 111 Avenue
Miami, Florida 33172
A PORTION OF THE SALE OF THIS BOOK WILL BE DONATED TO
POAT FOR THE CASTILLO AND HAWORTH FAMILIES.

Epilogue

This book was finished on January 15, 2011. When a book is finished, it is like closing a casket. One might think that the job is done, but does not want the casket to be closed anyway. I closed the casket on this book, but before it would go to press, the events on January 20th 2011 rocked the police world, and I was forced to reopen this book's manuscript.

The slaying of two police officers as they attempted to serve a warrant for murder in St. Petersburg stunned a state already mourning two police deaths in Miami, and capped a bloody twenty-four hours nationwide that saw eleven officers shot in five states. Another officer who had been shot would die on January 26th.

On January 20, 2011 Miami-Dade Police Officers Det. Roger Castillo, and Det. Amanda Haworth, lost their lives in the line of duty while trying to arrest an accused murderer. Four detectives from an elite unit went to try to arrest the killer. Their murderer was shot and killed by MDPD Detective Oscar Plasencio, but only after the suspect shot Howarth and Castillo each in the head. The angry, desperat,e twenty-three year-old was born and nursed when Howarth and Castillo were still in the police academy. MDPD Director James Loftus said that "one hundred years of experience went out that day; only fifty came back".

I attended the dual funeral, which took twelve hours. I was a member of the honor guard. The twelve horse, the eighteen boats, the dozen helicopters, the thousands of police officers, were small consolation to the four children who lost their respective parents. Thousands of police officers, resplendent in uniform shirts, brown, green, black, blue, grey, white, and tan, converged on the arena from NYPD, Boston, Chicago, LAPD, and everywhere in Florida. Police dispatchers, cadets, and explorers, mingled with federal, state, county and municipal cops to mourn.

The procession from the arena to the cemetery took an hour and a half. I had been in a lot of funeral processions, but this was the longest. What amazed me was the number of people lining Interstate 95 to wave, cheer, salute, and wave flags. I saw a high mileage old junker parked next to a ninety thousand dollar luxury Mercedes Benz, the owners of each standing next to their cars, saluting.

I saw blacks and whites and Hispanics, men and women, old and young, children and elderly, the filthy rich and the dirt poor. In the City of Miami, men without homes shuffled out of Camillus House to pay respects. We passed by Latino neighborhoods and saw people waving flags and holding signs. In the primarily Black Miami Gardens area, people stood on cars and waved and saluted. I saw an old homeless man in a wheelchair wrapped in an American flag, because he didn't have the strength to wave it. It was a wonderful sight.

This funeral took place a day before the 2011 Honor Guard Academy. This was a period of unparalleled gun violence against us. On the day of the Castillo-Howarth funeral, January 24, 2011, two officers in St. Petersburg, Florida were killed trying to serve a warrant. St. Petersburg Police Sgt. Thomas Baitinger and Officer Jeffrey Yaslowitz were gunned down by a man who later killed himself.

On January 28, 2011, the day of the funeral in St. Petersburg, the President of the Broward County Multi Agency Honor Guard, produced a short, poignant tribute to the downed officers for the students and instructors of the 2011 Honor Guard Academy, since we could not attend. A wreath was laid, a 3 round volley was fired by an 8 man shotgun team, "Taps" was played, and a piper piped Amazing Grace.

Also worth mentioning that month, on January 16, 2011 Officer Larry Nehasil, a southeastern Michigan police officer was shot to death in an exchange of gunfire with two burglary suspects, one of whom also died. On January 23, 2011 a man opened fire inside a Detroit police precinct, wounding four officers including a commander, before he was shot and killed by police. Officer David Moore, an Indianapolis police officer shot twice in the face during a weekend traffic stop, was declared brain-dead on January 26, 2011. Moore's murderer had opened fire, striking Moore four times, after the officer pulled over a car that had been reported stolen.

After an intense twelve hour long "schooling" that the Howarth-Castillo funeral provided, there followed a wonderful thirty-two hour Honor Guard Academy attended by officers from Florida, Tennessee, and Alabama. This academy was marred only by the Florida Highway Patrol having to leave to go to the St. Petersburg funerals.

I decided to "re-open the casket", and add photos, information, and this epilogue. It was painful, but not nearly as painful as losing all of these officers that evil January.

God bless you all, and wear your vest.

The Author

References

Arlington National Cemetery. (2011). *Taps*. Retrieved on January 5, 2011, from: http://www.arlingtoncemetery.net/Taps .htm

Chaucer, G. (1386). The Canterbury Tales. Prologue to "The Miller's Tale".

Department of the Army. (2003). Field Manual (FM) No. 7-21.13, "The Soldiers Guide". Washington, DC: Department of the Army. Retrieved on January 5, 2011, from: http://www.globalsecurity.org/military/library/policy/army/fm/7-21-13/index.html

Kübler-Ross, E. (2005). On Grief and Grieving: Finding the Meaning of Grief Through the Five Stages of Loss. New York: Scribner.

Kübler-Ross, E. (1969). *On Death and Dying.* New York: Scribner.

Lyrics to Amazing Grace. Retrieved on January 22, 2011 from: http://www.constitution.org/col/amazing_grace.htm

Lyrics to the minstrel boy. Retrieved on January 22, 2011 from: http://minstrelboy.blogspot.com/2005/03/lyrics-to-minstrel-boy.html

NLEOMF (2011). *Facts & Figures.* Retrieved on February 23, 2011 from: http://www.nleomf.org/facts/

NLEOMF. (2011). *Laverne Daniel Schulz.* Retrieved on January 5, 2011, from: http://www.nleomf.org/officers/search/search-results/laverne-daniel-schulz.html.

Seeber, J. (2008). *United States Flag Manual.* The Military Salute Project, MSP-08.   Retrieved on January 11, 2011, from: http://militarysalute.proboards45.com

Sheridan, K. (2006). Bagpipe Brothers. New Jersey: Rivergate Books.

TASER Foundation (2011). Retrieved on January 14, 2011, from: http://www.taserfoundation.org/Pages/donations.aspx

United States Code. Title 4 § 1. Flag; stripes and stars on.

United States Code. Title 4 § 2. Same; additional stars.

United States Code. Title 4 § 3. Use of flag for advertising purposes; mutilation of flag.

United States Code. Title 4 § 4. Pledge of allegiance to the flag; manner of delivery.

United States Code. Title 4 § 5. Display and use of flag by civilians; codification of rules and customs; definition.

United States Code. Title 4 § 6. Time and occasions for display.

United States Code. Title 4 § 7. Position and manner of display.

United States Code. Title 4 § 8. Respect for flag.

United States Code. Title 4 § 9. Conduct during hoisting, lowering or passing of flag.

United States Code. Title 4 § 10. Modification of rules and customs by President.

Villanueva, J. (2011). *24 Notes That Tap Deep Emotions*. Retrieved on January 5, 2011, from: http://www.west-point.org/Taps/Taps.html

Wellesz, E. (1957) The New Oxford History of Music. New York: Oxford University Press.

"Tous les jours à tous points de vue je vais de mieux en mieux"

"Every day in every way I am getting better and better"

~ Émile Coué

A Word About the Lake Erika Police Department

Lake Erika is a rural area. The Lake Erika Police Department has been around for over 100 years. The citizens love the Lake Erika Police Department. The annual Lake Erika Police Department Appreciation Day is so popular that everyone in town takes the day off.

The PD has never had an officer killed in the line of duty. Every year the police get a raise, and no one has ever been fired or written up. Retirement with full benefits happens at 20 years. The cops are among the highest paid in the country. There are no ticket quotas, and no one in the town ever speeds or breaks the law.

Officers are well trained and polite, they love their supervisors, and the Chief has been re-elected every year unopposed for over three decades. They have never had an officer-involved shooting.

There is no union, since the city aldermen simply give the cops whatever they want every year.

Each officer gets a new take-home car every year. The paper does a weekly column about how great the cops are. The crime rate is zero. Sometimes three generations of cops are on duty at the same time.

The Lake Erika PD has a terrific honor guard that trains every week. Restaurants never charge Lake Erika cops for meals, since they are like family, and you don't charge family, do you? Every kid in Lake Erika puts down in their "what I want to be when I grow up" papers – that they want to be Lake Erika cops. It sounds like a great place to work, doesn't it?

Too bad I made it all up for this book. Most people wouldn't want to do my job for a million bucks. Well friends, I do it for a lot less.

Stay safe out there.

The Author.

NOTES

NOTES

NOTES

NOTES

NOTES

NOTES

NOTES

NOTES

NOTES

NOTES

WHITE MOUNTAIN PUBLISHING CO.

MIAMI, FLORIDA